BEAUTIFUL NECESSITY

BEAUTIFUL NECESSITY
The art and meaning of women's altars

With 117 illustrations, 74 in color

Kay Turner

This book is my votive offering to Nancy Dean

ACKNOWLEDGMENTS

At my altar of gratitude, I give thanks for the inspiration
and encouragement provided by friends, family, colleagues,
and guides who have been most necessary to
the creation and completion of this book:
Mary Sanger; Mary Margaret Návar; Sra. Soledad "Chole"
Pescina; Lisa Graybill; Karen Dinitz; Nancy Dean; Belinda
Kremer; Pat Jasper and Texas Folklife Resources, Austin,
TX; Steve Zeitlin and Citylore, New York, NY; Nancy
Nusz and the Oregon Folklife Program/Oregon Historical
Society, Portland, OR; Joanna Labow; Mildred Potenza;
Katherine Sadler; Judith Gleason; Anne Lafferty; Joanne
Mulcahy; Kathy Vargas; Suzanne K. Seriff; the women of
Lady-Unique-Inclination-of-the Night; Gail Wallat; Randy
Conner and David Sparks; William G. Doty; Ann
Cvetkovich; Elizabeth Peterson; Edith Jean Turner; Helen
W. Halsey; James H. Turner; Barbara Turner; Richard
Bauman; Américo Paredes; Beverly Stoeltje; M. Jane Young;
and to the source of many blessings, the Virgin of San Juan.

PAGE 1: Dixie Friend Gay, *Red Goddess* (front and back
view), from her installation *Lair of the Goddess,* 1990.
PAGE 2: Women in the Texas-Mexican Melendez family
have dedicated this altar to Our Lady of Guadalupe.
PAGE 3: Connie Arismendi, *Milagro,* 1993.
PAGE 4: Nancy Azara, *Tree Altar,* 1994.
PAGE 5: Regina Vater, *Vervê* (1997), detail of installation.

First published in paperback in the United States of America in 1999 by
Thames & Hudson Inc., 500 Fifth Avenue, New York, New York 10110

Library of Congress Catalog Card Number 99-70846
ISBN 0-500-28150-5

Printed and bound in Slovenia

CONTENTS

INTRODUCTION

A PLACE APART

the tradition of women's altars

The age-old task of religious art has been to bridge the division between the sacred and mundane, the spiritual and the material, the Self and the Other. We now live in a time when this division is at its most extreme, but, from the very beginnings of human consciousness, a particular religious art form has assuaged the terror of separation by creating a special site to serve the human desire for relationship with unseen gods and spirits. We call that place an altar, a place set apart to house the images of powerful sacred beings, who by their presence there can be called upon for help and comfort. An altar makes visible that which is invisible and brings near that which is far away; it marks the potential for communication and exchange between different but necessarily connected worlds, the human and the divine.

The word 'altar' usually brings to mind the great high altars in churches and temples dedicated to God and ceremoniously tended by a priest, rabbi, or minister. But this book is concerned with a different kind of altar, one that is not male-determined or dogma-bound. It is an intimate altar, a home altar, made by a woman, and dedicated for her personal devotion to the deities she chooses. For the past twenty-five years I have engaged in research on domestic altars, a very old tradition practiced for thousands of years by women of different religious beliefs the world over. The home altar is ancient in its legacy and yet continues to this day.

A rich and relatively unexplored vein of women's history links the altar found in the dwellings of female-centered Çatal Hüyük in the fifth millennium BCE with a similar one depicted on a Minoan seal centuries later. That link is sustained in the altar at the entryway to Nefertiti's private chambers at Armana and also in the Jewish *mishkan*. The Greek hearth altar dedicated to Hestia continued in the Roman one devoted to Vesta. The altar to the Virgin Mary

Minoan seal showing a priestess with a triton shell before an altar displaying horns of consecration and vegetation. (From Gimbutas, 1982.)

OPPOSITE Filled with votive statues and flowers, this Texas-Mexican Catholic home altar was attended for forty years by Sra. Micaela Zapata.

Thirteenth-century domestic altar from Lucca, Italy, dedicated to the Virgin Mother.

occupying a niche in the home of a thirteenth-century woman of Lucca in Italy finds its counterpart in an Italian Catholic home in Brooklyn today. A Pakistani or Indian home in Detroit contains an altar where women serve the same Hindu deities that have been worshiped for centuries. The woman who currently practices Goddess Spirituality, venerating the Neolithic Great Goddess at her altar, recalls and reinvents an ancient tradition for modern times. A convert from Protestantism to Buddhism discovers the value of another domestic altar tradition. And perhaps the reader has also reverently established an altar in her own home.

Certainly there is great variation, but the link between women's altar traditions remains unbroken. In fact, I would venture to say that, throughout its long history, the woman's domestic altar all over the world has changed little in its basic religious intentions or in its aesthetic treatment. A Mexican-American woman's altar filled with statues of the Virgin and other saints does not look very different from an altar laden with Goddess figures found in the Early Cucuteni shrine of Sabatinovka (5000–3500 BCE). A Transylvanian table altar for ritual vessels is similar to the modern altar of a woman in Oregon. A contemporary artist's altar heaped with reproductions of the Great Goddess is not only a recapitulation of *her*story, but an affirmation of its continuing vitality. If the first altar made by a woman was created some 8000 years ago and the most recent is being assembled somewhere by a woman today, the remarkable thing is that there is a connection between them, a shared purpose in altar-making between that ancient progenitor and her twentieth-century inheritor. Exploring and affirming that connection is the aim of this book.

I didn't grow up with the tradition of home altars. Raised as a Presbyterian, I was taught that the veneration of images was suspect. And yet I was one of those children who kept a secret corner in the upstairs attic. There I made fetishes of a disparate array of objects: rocks and shattered robin's eggs, key chains, and pencil stubs, along with pictures of my childhood god, Roy Rogers.

Years went by. I outgrew my "attic altar," devoted myself to and then retreated from Christianity in the turmoil of the 1960s. Still, I never lost the sense that objects intuitively gathered together were a powerful means of meeting the sacred unknown.

My fascination with women's altars started with an experience I had in 1974 in Quetzaltenango, Guatemala. My friend Nancy and I were nearing the end of a year-long trip that we had impulsively, and somewhat haphazardly, undertaken to study the goddesses of pre-Colombian Mayan cultures. By this time we had very little money, and often found ourselves wandering the market place,

Horned Goddess (1998), made by Kanta Bosniak and Diane Porter Goff, recalls and reclaims the Neolithic Great Mother Goddess.

gazing with longing at food we couldn't afford to buy. We became friendly with a butcher, a formidable Quiche Maya woman named Virginia, who occasionally took pity on the hungry *gringas* by giving us her day's leftover sausages.

Soon we were visiting Virginia quite regularly. Our amiable talk often turned to religion because she was a Catholic with an exuberant devotion to the Virgin and we were novice but eager Goddess-worshipers. Our friendship grew through these discussions, and one day Virginia invited us to have dinner at the home she shared with her mother. As soon as we arrived, she insisted that we follow her down a dimly lit corridor. Dutifully we trailed after her, and at the end of the hallway we entered a glowing pink room. There before us, all by itself, stood a lavish altar table overflowing with statues and pictures of the Virgin Mary and various saints. Candles blazed in front of the images, and vases of fresh flowers filled the room with an aroma I can still recall today. On a carved bench, turned toward the center of the altar, Virginia then knelt down and offered a brief prayer for Nancy and me. I was enraptured, overwhelmed. I felt that I had never seen anything so inspired or so perfect as this altar. Later that evening as we dined, I ventured to ask Virginia why she kept an altar at home, and she simply replied that it was "a beautiful necessity." She made no further explanation; I did not further inquire. But the phrase "a beautiful necessity," and the altar to which it referred, had captured me, and the mystery of its meaning began to grow in me.

After that first encounter, I began to see women's personal altars everywhere in my travels. I saw them in Mexico; I saw them in Italy; I saw them in the United States in Brooklyn, San Antonio, Albuquerque and Detroit. They were in the homes of Mexican Americans, Polish-Americans, and Vietnamese-Americans. And as the second wave of feminism and the first streams of gay liberation spilled out on to the cultural landscape I also found altars in the homes of middle-aged lesbians in Ohio and in the studios of radical feminist artists in New York.

Hindu home altar, *c.* 18th–19th century, with images of Krishna and Radha.

It was such a ubiquitous tradition, and, no matter where I observed it, the home altar was maintained predominantly almost exclusively—by women. I could not escape that simple fact—and for me its implications. Yet, in the early days of my interest, I found very little documentation to support my growing sense of the tradition's importance. Anthropological and art-historical sources either failed to mention home altars or described them in terms that always implied their insignificance. I remember, for example, reading George Foster's classic ethnography of Tzintzuntzan, Mexico. Even though he found that "every home has one or more simple altars," he dismissed them as a kind of "low-pitched daily homage" and said no more.[1] Typically neglected or obscured, this woman's way of knowing the Divine seemed weighted by its absence from history. I knew I had a mission. And my urgency only grew as in 1975 I began to assemble fragments of the tradition's history that did exist.

Certainly, as the bibliography for this book attests, the available literature on domestic altars has grown considerably since I began my study years ago. A detailed, cross-cultural historical treatment remains to be done, but for my purpose here even a brief review of the evidence in the Western archaeological and historical record alone reveals certain themes that recur consistently in women's altar-making from the distant past to the present. I should forewarn the reader in acknowledging that my research focuses on the pre-Christian and Christian—specifically Catholic—history of the tradition in the West. Other religious

Shrine of Sabatinovka (Early Cucuteni Culture, 5000–3500 BCE, Southern Bug Valley, Moldavia). Interior shows a clay altar littered with Goddess figurines and a throne near the altar where an officiant may have been seated. (From Gimbutas, 1982.)

Reconstruction of a cult table supporting ritual vessels, classical Petresti settlement at Pianul de Jos, Transylvania, mid-fifth millennium, BCE. (From Gimbutas, 1982.)

Vessels and ritual instruments on Margallee James's contemporary home altar recall its ancient and continuing purpose as a place of libation, offering and prayer.

cultures which maintain legacies of the domestic altar tradition—Buddhist and Hindu, for example—deserve further consideration which is not possible here.

The first Western domestic altars were made in the Neolithic era around 5000–6000 BCE. In many pre-patriarchal cultures in Old Europe, the Near East, the Indus Valley, and the Mediterranean, altars were dedicated in households to insure the protection and advocacy of various life-giving and life-nourishing fecund goddesses. The veneration of their images, most likely initiated and certainly sustained by women (as, for example, the record at Çatal Hüyük indicates), formed the ideological core of early matrifocal (mother-centered) religions, shaped by reverence for fertility, reproduction, and regeneration—in a word, creativity—and asserting the interconnection between all things, animate and inanimate.

Across cultures, early domestic altars exhibit similar features in their construction: a low platform used as a base to assemble votive images of deities—female figures generally outnumbering male—accompanied by ritual objects, such as pottery incense-burners, lamps, and offering-vessels. These altars were sacred settings where libation, offering, prayer, adoration, petition, and propitiation combined to create daily and seasonal cycles of communication with the divine feminine, the Creatrix.

The archaeologist Marija Gimbutas is renowned for her recovery and interpretation of Goddess-centered religious culture in many societies in Old Europe. She suggests that the art of these early societies shows the persistent and widespread use of altars, images, figures, symbolic script, graphic design, and ritual accouterments in formulating what she calls a "language of the goddess," a language for abstract ideas. The home altar was no doubt the place where this language, based on representation and analogy, was primarily "spoken" over thousands of years. At their altars women repeatedly engaged in combining religious objects and ideas, uniting the material and the spiritual in an exploration of consciousness itself and in the subsequent formulation of values for human living.

At the very core of the domestic altar tradition's purpose is an age-old concern for mediating the gap between Self and Other in a specifically woman-centered way. If a mother recognized that the child born from her body was both of and separate from her, "the language of the goddess" translated this physical fact into a powerful recognition of both the differences and similarities between Self and Other, and ways of mediating the two through acts of ritual communication and care. The Goddess housed on her altar acted as a cognitive stimulus, a template. She presented a model of maternity, with references not only to the biology of motherhood (and its associated physical manifestations, such as menstruation and lactation), but also to ideas and beliefs that made up a formative maternal ideology concerned with generation and regeneration, birth and rebirth, giving and receiving, being and not being.

These cycles were understood within the context of maternal practices—of giving birth, nurturing, and raising children—and a kind of embodied thinking, a thinking through the sacred representation of the female body. Judy Grahn, in her important amplification of Gimbutas's findings, suggests that "Goddess icons embody ideas as the primary motive for their existence." They are what she calls "metaforms," "containers of ideas," and she argues that "the connection of woman to nature, as reflected in art, is a cultural connection; that is to say our ancestors expressed relationships with other creatures in order to give form to their ideas."[2] In the making of their altars, our ancient foremothers were engaged in a profound revolution: the invention of a place where the idea and value of relationship was born. A reverence for shared images and symbols first gave rise to the meaning of shared relationship with the sacred female Other, and at the same time with all others—humans, animals, plants—who dwelled together in the first creation of community.

Cultures of the Goddess and her domestic altars were transformed and diminished, but never fully obliterated, as patriarchal rule and religions evolved and consolidated in early Western societies over a two-thousand-year period beginning, roughly, in the third millennium BCE. Riane Eisler defines this paradigm shift to patriarchy as the movement from the "partnership model" to the "dominator model" of society and culture. The culture of ancient Greece provides insight into this transformation. As the Greek state evolved from 1000 to 200 BCE, patriarchal ascendancy produced social, philosophical, and religious polarities along gender lines (polarities which still determine gender hierarchies in the West today), including the distinction between *polis* (state/public/male) and *oikos* (household/private/female). Patriarchy re-configured the Self-Other relationship from one of complement to opposition: "woman" became the devalued "Other" dominated by the prescriptions of "man," the ideal "Self." A culture of kings, heroes, and wars—of male superiority first assumed in assigning women to an inferior status—developed and finally triumphed. Female-centered domestic worship was marginalized as public temples grew in imperial importance. But the powers of primal fertility and Greek family legacy still emanated from the household in reverence for Hestia, goddess of the hearth altar.

Her significance is remarked in the Greek proverb, "Begin with Hestia," for it was said that she "is enthroned in the middle of the universe, just as the hearth is at the center of the house."[3] The etymology of Hestia's name reveals her importance: *ousia* is glossed as "substance, primary, real, the substratum underlying all change and process," and its most common derivative is *estia*, defined as "a hearth, a household or family, an altar."[4] In Hestia's name is the root form for the very meaning of "essential being"or "essential reality." Further, her virginity confirmed her self-generating, self-sustaining powers. At the center of the family, Hestia stood as an image of inviolate privacy reflecting "the idea of conserving, withholding, and keeping internal the basic elements of the support system, the household."[5] Hestia was a woman's goddess. Even as women's power was being occluded by patriarchal ascendancy, Hestian devotion marked women's religious autonomy and consequent self-identity.

Women celebrated the sanctity of the hearth and their alliance with Hestia in ritual acts, including daily food offerings and ceremonies such as the *amphidromia*, an inaugural carrying of newborn children around the hearth to welcome them into the home.[6] Ensuring the female legacy of the hearth altar was at the core of the Greek wedding ceremony. Lighting a torch from the fire of her own hearth, the bride's mother then carried it ahead of the newly married couple and lit their first household fire with hers.[7]

A Greek stela, *c.* 500 BCE, shows Mother Goddess Demeter and her daughter Persephone making ritual gestures over the fire of a small altar.

Hestia is a crucial figure in the historic lineage of the domestic altar; she is the key to an understanding of the tradition, still important today, as a testament to what feminist theologian Christine Downing calls the "holiness of the ordinary." Downing says that Hestia provokes a question: "She creates suspicion of the extraordinary, of all that we usually mean by the divine."[8] She demarcates a crucial difference between her realm and all other sacred sites: one need go no farther from the holy than home. At a turning point in Western history, when patriarchal exclusion of women in many public religious domains became socially established, Hestia and her hearth altar gave validity to an approach to religion that remained female-centered, private, personal, self- and family-connected. The value of a woman's difference—her reproductive and maternal capability, but moreover her autonomy and sense of self-worth—were placed in the keeping of a tradition that quite simply would not let go.

The etymology of our word "altar," in fact, reflects this division. It is derived from the Latin *altus*, meaning high, and refers to a raised structure for the presentation of offerings to deities. Once temples had been established as the formal habitation of the gods, the Greeks and later the Romans distinguished the high temple altar (*altare*), dedicated to the honor of a supreme, often a state god, from the domestic hearth altar (*focus*). Temple altars were the sites of public sacrifice and official celebration; domestic altars were reserved as a place to focus family and individual attention on the gods. Aligned with the powers of home and hearth, the domestic altar remained a place of origin, generation, and regeneration. And most assuredly it was a woman's source of focus for her understanding of the Divine. As state and imperial religions exalted in transcendence, women's sense of the religious retained its basis in immanence.

That a woman-centered domestic altar tradition played a part in the beginnings of Christianity is far from merely speculative. This new religion was troubled by its conflict with long-established state and pagan traditions; for example, the Roman temple to Isis, whose religion was considered most favorable to women, was still active until 300 CE. Initially, the Church was driven underground, and surreptitious worship quite likely required some features of the domestic altar cult. Scholars suggest that in the first two centuries women formed a core group, coming into early Christianity from other traditions. In fact, Celsus, an early critic, denounced Christianity as a religion of marginals: women, children, and slaves. Celsus exaggerates his point, but probably women enjoyed a certain centrality and perhaps some unfettered creativity in the first years of the Church. They had enough power, no doubt, to bring their familiarity with pagan forms of domestic devotion into the secret rites of the newly evolving faith.

Centuries later, when patriarchal Christianity had become the dominant religion in the West, the home altar still gave women a special place for developing their religious values. Encaustic portrait images of the saints, and of Christ and Mary began to be made in the fifth century, and it is thought that painted icons were originally created for home use.[9] Like their pagan counterparts, early Christian images were treated with a sense of individual affiliation. Faith in the living power of images fueled both their veneration and petition for personal help, favor, and blessing—they were not merely static representations of a power that dwelt elsewhere.[10] Belief in icons was highly attractive to women. They could appeal to images without intervention from the Church hierarchy, which offered women limited participation in public worship. The Church Fathers condemned women's "superstitious" devotions, but, as historian Judith Herrin suggests, "The cult of icons provided a suitable vehicle for the expression of female religiosity, being a very personal one which could be practiced privately…. For those who owned domestic icons, there were no restrictions on their devotions…."[11] Herrin notes that home altars were a feature of Byzantine life. And while it is true that both men and women used them, she claims that women had the strongest reasons for promoting private domestic worship.

Eventually, a political conflict, the iconoclast controversy of the eighth century, broke out between those who claimed the efficacy of unmediated personal relationship with images and those who did not. The iconoclast clergy, in an attempt to consolidate their power, contended that, "only objects that had been properly blessed by the appropriate authority could be treated as holy."[12] Privately worshiped icons were not formally blessed, and, unsurprisingly, women were more likely to be iconophiles (devotees of icons), even risking the censure and rage of their iconoclast husbands. Powerful women of the Byzantine Empire struggled, often subversively, to retain their right to venerate personal images at their altars. While the Emperor Theophilus publicly condemned the worship of images and persecuted the worshipers, the Empress Theodora and her mother-in-law Euphrosyne secretly continued their veneration of icons—and taught such devotion to their children—in the private women's quarters of the palace.[13] The end of iconoclasm was itself precipitated by a woman. After the death of her iconoclast husband, Leo IV, Irene became regent in the year 780, and immediately reinstated the cult of images.[14]

In the Western Roman Catholic world, following the split from Constantinople in 1054, private devotion and the demand for images continued to increase during medieval times. Around 1300 devotional images to accompany private prayer began to be more widely distributed throughout Europe.[15] Increasingly, the cheap manufacture of mold-made images, engravings, and even small altars gave people from all classes greater domestic access to the Divine.

Small, mass-produced home altar depicting *The Adoration of the Magi*. Painted walnut with lead tracery and rosettes, and stamped paper backgrounds. South Netherlandish (Brussels), *c.* 1500–20.

By the thirteenth century the cult of the Virgin Mary had taken precedence over all others, and continued unabated for over three hundred years. During this time images of the Virgin in painting and sculpture became much more human, subjective, and emotionally wide-ranging. Her earthly, bodily life was stressed in realistic images that centered thematically on her role as Virgin Mother. Scenes of the Annunciation were often shown taking place in contemporary domestic settings. Other popular images, including those of Mary suckling the infant Christ, or portraying her relationship with her mother, St. Anne, confirmed Mary's ultimate "humanity" inscribed in her maternity, but also demonstrated her influence in Christ's earthly destiny and her autonomy within a female lineage of support.

Unfortunately, at the same time that visual messages of the powerful immanence of the Virgin came to dominate the production of images for the Church, verbal messages pronouncing the innate inferiority of women were very much a part of Catholic theology. The contrast, however, leaves room for suggesting, as feminist religious scholar Margaret Miles has done,[16] that women's personal interpretations of visual images may have provided a strategy for self-empowerment over and against verbal misogyny. Visual images can provide a wider range of personally interpreted meanings than texts can. Miles assumes, for example, that images of Mary's virginity, which were for churchmen non-threatening testimonies to her purity and passivity, could have been integrated by women into an understanding of her freedom from the entailments of marriage and sexuality, and hence her spiritual autonomy. Miles makes a crucial, if speculative, claim for women's interpretation of images as indicative of the "creative intelligence of medieval women and their ability to work for their own advantage with images they did not control."[17] A woman's personal altar was the obvious setting for her subversive interpretations of relationship with divine allies such as the Virgin, Mary Magdalene, St. Anne, and others who would understand and abet her needs and her wishes.

The altar as a site of subversion is also linked, no doubt, to women's interconnectedness with each other through the practice of the tradition. Both within families and communities, women's reliance on a network of religious affiliations—official and unofficial—gave them a means for trying to fulfill their own needs. Under patriarchy, women have always worked creatively to benefit from their shared resources, and in religious terms this has often resulted in a process of hybridization between older pagan or primal religious traditions with evolving state or institutional religions. In the Middle Ages, for example, women who sought refuge from patriarchy in their private devotion to the Virgin and saints also had recourse to the supernatural gifts of midwives, healers and diviners—witches—whose altars joined the natural and magical with the cultural and doctrinal. Marginalized practitioners of the old earth-based religions combined Catholicism with herbal medicine, amulets, potions, incantations, blessings, and curses to produce real effects—a birth, a healing, a miracle—in a world that allowed women little power. This mixing of elements from old and new religions is central to an understanding of women's altar traditions because historically it has always been women who are more likely to keep or reinvigorate old practices alongside the new, which are usually a result of male-determined war, conquest, or ideological transformations.

Overall, the history of women's home altars under patriarchy can be fruitfully viewed within the larger framework of women's culture, a concept used by feminist historians to denote a culture distinct from but operating within the general culture that is shared by both men and women. This concept distinguishes activities, beliefs, and behaviors which are generated out of women's lives from those roles and behaviors prescribed for them.[18] As the feminist historian Gerda Lerner has stated: "Women live their social existence within the general culture and, whenever they are confined by patriarchal restraint or segregation into separateness (which always has subordination as its purpose), they transform this restraint into complementarity (asserting the importance of woman's function, even its 'superiority') and redefine it. Thus, women live a duality—as members of the general culture and as partakers of women's culture."[19] Where such "living in duality" exists—and it exists widely—women's beliefs and attitudes are expressed through ritual and art, providing a visible focus for the validation of women's contributions to culture as a whole or as expressions of their conflict with the dominant culture. The home altar,

Joos van Cleve's
The Annunciation, c. 1525,
depicts the Virgin Mary as
a typically devout sixteenth-
century Dutch woman. Her
bedchamber features a
half-opened triptych-style
altar with an engraving of
Christ pinned on the wall
next to it.

for example, has for centuries encoded a visual language through which objects "speak" to the distinctive concerns of women's "hidden" culture.

Visible traces of the domestic altar in the historical record reveal not only the fact of its existence, but also the way in which a women's religious and artistic tradition, uninterrupted and evolving over time, can be said to mark the maintenance of certain tenacious, even unyielding, values. The altar is a material expression of values; influence, not simply representation, is its final end. Perhaps even a partial and "voiceless" history, as briefly summarized here, suggests the great legacy that the home altar retains in the many versions of its practice today. That legacy points to the continuing validity of a religious tradition which expresses certain crucial aspects of women's interpretation of living. Fertility, maternity, birth and rebirth, family generation and social regeneration, creativity, sacred embodiment of the feminine, the Self-Other relationship, self-identity, and autonomy are concerns and values consistently addressed at women's home altars worldwide. Taken together, they enfold a feminine paradigm of co-creation favoring a particular understanding of the union of body and spirit. If this paradigm was central to the formation of human society, and then marginalized under patriarchy, it was always given visible recognition in the tradition of home altars.

This brief history is a starting point for the rest of this book, which is devoted to the current practice of the tradition, and, thankfully, replaces speculation with direct evidence: the living voices of women speaking to the meaning of personal altars in their lives. In 1979, for my dissertation, I started interviewing Mexican-American women in South Texas. Over the course of several years, they became my foremost teachers in their versions of the folk-Catholic altar tradition. Eventually, I began questioning altar-makers wherever I encountered them, and in 1983 I published a special issue on the diversity of women's altars in *Lady-Unique-Inclination-of-the-Night*, the feminist spirituality journal that I edited at the time. Since then I have continued to pursue the tradition in all its variety of expression throughout the United States. For me, this book is very much like an altar on which I have gathered together portraits of so many of those women, some of whom I have now known for decades. Their grace and insight, shared with me in often lengthy interviews, are necessarily distilled here, but—I hope—without diluting the knowledge and experience that each has brought to my understanding of women's altars. Their testimony in these pages typifies the legions of women in the past and present whose keeping of the tradition lays claim to its beautiful necessity.

Most women, including many I have known, maintain altars within the context of folk-religious practices associated with but often running counter to institutionalized religions, such as Catholicism. In class- and gender-stratified societies, folk religion harbors and generally exercises an autonomy based on symbols and rituals that favor the subjective, individual aspects of religion. Keeping an altar is one of many folk-religious traditions that over centuries have been of benefit to women excluded from full participation in male-dominated religions. But in the late twentieth century, altar-making has grown dramatically, has even erupted, at a time when established religions are no longer central in the lives of many women. Unaffiliated Pagans, Wiccans, and Goddess-worshipers have taken the tradition for themselves, reclaiming and reinventing it for these new times. Artists, too, have been drawn to it. They bring the private altar into public settings, fluidly combining images and materials to reveal essential aspects of the tradition in startling new ways.

Contemporary altar-makers range from the very traditional to the radically revisionist, and I have tried to include representatives of them all. Sra. Soledad "Chole" Pescina, a Texas-Mexican Catholic, learned altar-making over a hundred years ago from her grandmother in Mexico, and every day, until her death in 1986 at the age of ninety, tended and used her altar dedicated to Nuestra Señora de Guadalupe (Our Lady of Guadalupe) and San Antonio (St. Anthony). In contrast, the artist Kathy Vargas works within her Mexican tradition, but radically renews it by creating photographically based altars dedicated to the memory or aid of dear friends. Traditional altars built to invite the presence of Afro-Atlantic gods and goddesses, such as Ogún and Yemayá, are made by Miriam Chamani, founder of the Voodoo Spiritual Temple at her home in New Orleans. Yet Ogún is also given a central place on the new home altar of Candice Goucher, a professor of African history living in Portland, Oregon. Artists expand both the interpretation of the altar for women and its visual aesthetic by transforming aspects of its history, sometimes by appropriating ancient symbols and giving them a very contemporary slant, or by inventing new symbols which are sacralized by enclosing them in the altar's frame. The artist Nancy Blair creates reproductions of ancient goddess figures for women's altars all over the world, while another artist, Nancy Fried, diagnosed with breast cancer, makes terracotta altars of breasts dedicated to her own healing. These and many others presented here show that, although cultural and individual histories play their part in determining particular practices, it might also be said that we are united as women in our various altar traditions.

This deeply historical and widely dispersed religious art form provokes questions concerning the different meaning of women's beliefs, values, and creativity. Perhaps more than any other domestic art form, the personal altar demonstrates the validity of identifying the distinctive features of a feminist aesthetic. I think of how much we've learned about women's creativity and social expertise from the feminist study of the quilt. By linking feminist theory to the history of quilting, scholars brought fresh perspectives to a range of quilt-makers' concerns—family legacy, creativity, and social networks—that were unthought of twenty years ago. A feminist approach to altars similarly provides the opportunity to probe women's spiritual-aesthetic concerns for answers to deeper questions about the meaning of feminine creativity, not in limiting essentialist terms but as a concept that bridges women's distinctive bodily and psychological determinations with their experience and values. In fact, my interpretation of women's altars tries to demonstrate a point of reconciliation in the long-standing feminist debate that opposes essentialism and social construction. Our altars do make a claim on women's difference from men, but not simply as a natural cause, rather as an ethical and therefore a socially invested one that asserts a woman's perspective on the meaning of life lived in the union of body, spirit and intelligence, not in their separation.

Why has the home altar survived the passage from pre-patriarchy to patriarchy and now to what is hopefully an evolving post-patriarchal era? What is so central to the tradition, no matter how or where it appears, that has kept it vitally entrenched for millennia? The answer to these questions is not a simple one, but my overall sense is that the home altar consecrates and serves women's understanding of the *power of relationship* to overcome separation with an emphasis on the values of inclusion and exchange. The home altar is a visible representation of this power, and a highly effective instrument for bringing it into action and effect. Even if, by definition, all altars perpetuate an affiliation with the Divine, women's altars promote a particular ideal of relationship and approve its fundamental continuity within women's lived experience.

In the past several decades feminist scholars have worked broadly on the crucial meaning of relationship for women. My understanding of women's altars owes much to the writings of medievalist Caroline Walker Bynum, art critic Lucy Lippard, psychologist Carol Gilligan, theologian Carol Ochs, and archaeologist Marija Gimbutas. In their own areas of expertise, they and many others have articulated a relational perspective on women's difference. Asserting the gendered nature of all religious experience, Bynum claims, "Religious experience is the experience of men and women, and in no known society is this experience the same." Her study of medieval European religious writers suggests that women are more likely to build religious metaphors from social and biological experiences, and that their use of symbols is "given to the muting of opposition." She also finds in medieval women's use of religious symbols a "tendency to emphasize reconciliation and continuity."[20] Bynum's remarks are particular to a historical period, yet this "tendency" is, I think, also in evidence in women's personal altars, sites where religious metaphors are most specifically assigned their intention by women. Altars symbolically convey women's concern for reconciliation, continuity, and the muting of opposition.

Anthropologists Judith Hoch-Smith and Anita Spring have also explored female religious metaphors. Women across cultures, to a consistent degree, are regarded as sacred primarily in connection with reproduction and mothering, and, following from this, with their skills in nurturing and relationships. Religious rituals and other practices sponsored by women on behalf of women often make creative use of the metaphors of menstruation, pregnancy, birth, lactation, and mother-child symbiosis to push the ideological precept beyond the production of the child to the creation and maintenance of human relationships.[21] Though not exclusively concerned with reproductive metaphors, the home altar tradition seeks divine help in initiating, preserving, restoring, and protecting the vitality of all relationships.

Sociologists Kathryn March and Rachelle Taqqu invite a closer inspection of religious domains, such as altars, where "women actively exercise their authority as women within a divinely sanctioned interpretation of their gender rights."[22] They argue that private religious activities do not necessarily rationalize women's place in the wider spheres of sex-stratified societies, but may serve as a "legitimate basis for autonomous action" emerging at least in part "from the supposedly 'affective' basis of [women's] shared cultural perceptions."[23] Women's religious competence arises from feeling, intuition, emotion, and simply from the experience of being a woman.

Carol Ochs suggests that women's spirituality "focuses on something that is available to all people equally—their own experience," and is "the process of coming into relationship with reality." According to Ochs, women's reality—and hence our sense of spirituality—is based on the female model of development that gives priority to relationship and interconnectedness.[24] Women's spiritual disposition favors a reality that is patterned by obligation, care, and responsibility to others and to themselves. Every day women proclaim the value of this reality at their altars. In the intimacy of their own homes, in the presence of a sacred site that they themselves have created, women do not seek salvation *from* this world; rather, they find a more productive, integrated sense of relationship *with* this world—and those who dwell in it.

Twenty-five years ago, at the beginning of second-wave feminist revisions of religion, Mary Daly spoke of the need for women to create a new space apart, a space which she defined as a state of mind "where it is possible to be oneself, without the contortions of mind, will, feeling, and imagination demanded of women by sexist society." Further, she held that this new space cannot be "static space"; rather, it must be "constantly moving space…its center is on the boundaries of patriarchy's spaces, that is, it is not contained."[25] Daly's idea of a dynamic "space apart" is prefigured in the domestic altar, a woman's place apart, built and maintained for centuries before patriarchy, and then conserved for centuries more on the boundaries of patriarchal alienation. Deep within her home the woman's private altar has been—and continues to be—a self-made sanctuary dedicated to the fulfillment of her own *gyno-theology*.

CHAPTER ONE

PREPARING A PLACE
defining the personal altar

A woman's personal altar evokes her particular—her intimate—relationship to the divine, human, and natural realms. There she assembles a highly condensed, symbolic model of connection by bringing together sacred images and ritual objects, pictures, mementos, natural materials, and decorative effects which represent different realms of meaning and experience—heaven and earth, family and deities, nature and culture, Self and Other. By actively engaging the Divine at this self-created sacred place, she makes her altar a living instrument of communication, a channeling device for integration, reconciliation, and creative transformation.

Women come to the altar tradition in many ways: some through legacy, some through conversion, others intuitively or through conscious self-invention. Among all the women's altars I have seen, no two look exactly the same, nor are used in exactly the same way. Each one reflects the individuality of its maker; its conventional elements, candles and pictures of deities, for instance, are always wedded to a creative impulse. The home altar exists at a point of intersection between art and religion where the sacred is apprehended in a woman's *imagined* relationship with the Divine. Imagination in this sense is the development of a relationship to religious images and symbols that requires no legitimization, no "outside" approval. Ultimately, the home altar—its look, its feel, its intention—is hers alone. And yet the altar practice tends towards certain universal principles. It engages women's history, women's beliefs, and women's desires at a level of common association that can only be confirmed by allowing altar-makers to speak directly about the meaning of the tradition for them.

In the years since I began this study, I have regularly asked women to define the personal altar as they view it and use it. They stress its importance and purpose, and show an understanding both of the legacy of the tradition and its

Bereniece Alvarado devoted her altar to Our Lady of Guadalupe, as did her mother. Sra. Alvarado positioned her altar above her bed so she could "find" the Virgin immediately upon rising each day.

Soledad "Chole" Pescina's folk-Catholic altar tradition was learned from her Mexican grandmother over 100 years ago.

current power. One of the first altar-makers I ever interviewed was Sra. Soledad "Chole" Pescina, an elderly Catholic Mexican-American who rarely went to church because, as she once asserted, "We are our own priests at home." From her grandmother in Mexico, Chole learned a female-based folk Catholicism, the center of which was the home altar: "Why do you have an altar in your home? Because you got it from the religion taught to you by your parents. And you follow the tradition. It's an ancient tradition and you can't get away from it, wherever you go...." Chole claimed the home altar as an expression of women's distinctive religious power; it confirmed her sense that, "Women value different things than men." Sra. Micaela Zapata, her old friend and neighbor down the block, felt much the same way. In distinguishing the church altar from hers at home, she insisted, "These *altarcitos* (personal altars) belong to us women."

As these traditional altar-keepers suggest, ownership of an altar is a means of women's survival. Shamaan Ochaum, a healer and therapist, concurs: "I guess basically for me, a home is not a home unless you have a sacred site there. That's the first thing I have to find for myself.... I have to have a sacred site, a place where I can go to touch inside of me and connect to the womb of the universe. For me, that's a life issue...a way of surviving. When I open the door to my meditation room where my altar is, an immediate peace comes over me.... There is a certain tranquillity that is always in that room because there has only been meditation and prayer there. Seeking. Communing. And the minute I see the altar—I know it's a place where I get healed, replenished,

and comforted…. It doesn't replace so much as it amplifies. It amplifies something that is already inside of me. The thing that is already inside of me is a recognition of divinity, an acknowledgment of divinity in myself, in the earth, in nature, and in others."

The material objects of an altar and their condensed arrangement promote the kind of spiritual amplification Shamaan defines as the altar's purpose. Along with the basic assumption of an altar as "sacred space," it is this sense of heightened attention that many women speak of in describing the usefulness of the personal altar. Artist Requa Tolbert says, " It is a place to concentrate spiritual power and experience. It is a thing I craft with my hands *and* heart *and* head…. It is a focal point for placing intention, and a distillation of the beauty I recognize in my home, my land, and my family."

The focus an altar provides is lent to engagement with the Divine. An altar is a place between divine and human realms, a threshold charged with exchange which writer Cristina Biaggi calls: "The meeting place of the sacred and the mundane; the parenthesis between the two worlds…where communication with the ineffable is possible…. Altars are very important tools used for facilitating the interweaving of the two worlds." Similarly, artist Regina Vater says, "The altar is a threshold, a threshold of contact with another dimension that is here all the time…. The sacred place makes the connection." And Celtic-inspired Pagan, Sharynne NicMacha, maintains that, "an altar puts my attention, here in the physical plane, on the spiritual nature, or unseen, side of things. It is the physical manifestation of how I view the spiritual world."

ABOVE LEFT Sharynne NicMacha follows a pagan Celtic altar tradition, which blends veneration of natural elements with devotion to goddesses such as Brigit and Macha and the god Cernunnos.

ABOVE RIGHT Shamaan Ochaum seated before her welcoming altar, which serves as a spiritual greeting place for guests and a focus of family ritual.

An altar is very much a "between" place, a meeting place where invisible powers are given material form; the material is made to serve the spiritual and vice versa. Eclipse, a teacher of ritual arts, suggests that, "Altar-building is a creative process where ancient power and personal objects come together in the same space, creating a gateway to another realm." Defining the altar as a threshold or gateway is important for understanding its potential to serve a woman's own religious concerns. A threshold is also a point of departure; it is exuberant with the dynamism of change and choice. It evokes *cathexis:* the discharge of desire. A woman's altar, her self-created threshold, exists between the physical and the spiritual, and exists, moreover, between her sense of belief and her sense of need. Every approach to her altar activates a woman's desire for fulfillment, her desire to cross the gap between the Self and the Other for her own purposes. Artist Rose Wognum Frances affirms, "Altar-making is a choice to keep your spiritual life alive on a daily basis, to surround yourself with it, immerse yourself in it and immerse yourself in the beauty of it, the objects of it, the image of it, the community of it…. If you keep that path alive, altar-making is a wonderful way to have that path unfold."

For a woman, keeping an altar is a distinctly personal assumption of relationship with divine allies in whatever form they take for her. For many raised traditionally—for example, in Catholic, Eastern Orthodox, or Hindu homes—the altar legacy is maternal in origin; personal relationship with divine beings is a gift from grandmothers or mothers to their daughters. Sra. Consuelo "Chelo" Gonzalez received the centerpiece of her altar in the form of an image of Our Lady of Guadalupe, the patron saint of Mexico, given to her by her mother shortly before she died: "It's an inheritance that my mother has left me—also a faith in the Virgin of Guadalupe that is very great." Born in 1899 and raised a Roman Catholic, Sra. Bereniece Alvarado also inherited her mother's faith: "I have more devotion to Our Lady of Guadalupe…. My mother had a lot of devotion to Our Lady of Guadalupe. She had a lot. Me, too." Sra. Alvarado's devotion is also maternal in its concerns. Her living-room altar features an image of Our Lady of Guadalupe placed above portraits of her twelve children. She says simply, but with conviction: "She's as much their mother as I am."

In contrast, Aina Olomo, a practitioner in the African-based *orisha* tradition, received her relationship with Shangó, the god of thunder, at the end of a complex, year-long initiation. Her altar to Shangó is in a room by itself where he "sits" in the sacred pot that Aina was given at initiation to "house" him with her until death. "That's where he lives. I go to his altar and consult with him there in my room.... I have Shangó in heaven, in the elements. And then I have Shangó in my head. And then I have him in there, in my room. The goal is for all those to be lined up. To realize the strength of that oneness." Another altar-maker Shelley Anderson states: "As a woman, I worship the Goddess because I cannot do otherwise. The image on my altar is of the Buddhist goddess Kwan Yin, the Compassionate One, She Who Listens to the Cries of the World. She is a *bodhisattva*, a being who chooses to return to this world in order to help other beings achieve liberation. She is a daily reminder of the power of listening, of bearing witness to suffering—and of the power inherent in women to fight the forces that cause oppression."

Annapurna is a devout convert to SRV (The Sarada Ramakrishna Vivekananda Association), a Western sect of Hinduism. She says: "My only interest is in realizing God—with form and without—which means that all life must be seen as divinity manifested, all actions, all objects. The altar evokes the Divine Presence...we are encouraged to keep it very sacred. Ideally the altar is located in a room that serves no other purpose. No worldly (mundane) activities should take place there and we should strive to keep out mundane thoughts as well—the way we keep it pure externally should be reflected in our minds. This is easier said than done.... But ultimately, feeling the Presence in an altar and in sacred objects is the training to feel so wherever we are. This is a Hindu-style altar and it is for our whole association, not just for me, personally. It is dedicated to Sarada, Ramakrishna, and Swami Vivekananda, specifically, and to Divine Mother in Her forms of Kali and Durga, generally, because we see S, R, and V as the triple descent of Kali in this age."

Folklorist Sabina Magliocco practices Wicca, a revitalized tradition of witchcraft that focuses devotion on manifestations of the Goddess and the God. For Wiccans, the altar is foremost a setting for the tools that are ritually used to invoke blessing and change: "Revival Witchcraft is a religion which is part of a larger movement called Neo-Paganism, an attempt to revive, recreate, and experiment with ancient forms of polytheistic worship. Witches trace their heritage to a European magical tradition which they believe is a survival of pagan religions practiced by the ancestors of contemporary northern Europeans and Euro-Americans.... In its most basic form, the Wiccan altar is a place to put sacred tools during a ritual. Some Witches keep standing altars in their homes where they perform rituals on a regular basis, engage in meditation and other forms of worship. Rituals may also be constructed for a particular purpose, for example, to honor one particular deity, or to serve as a focal point for energy and magical work for one particular purpose.... An altar serves as a focal point for energy in private devotion, celebration, spell-work, healing. It holds ritual tools such as salt, water, candles, and representations of deities; it can hold objects which evoke certain qualities for the practitioner.... Many Witches...feel that in theory the altar is optional.... An altar can be made anywhere—since deity is immanent in this religion—on the ground..., at the base of a tree, in a hotel room. An altar is not necessary for either magic or worship, since the tools for that are inside us all; but it is helpful because magic works best when we can raise and focus emotions and energy, and symbols are important tools in that process. You need a place to put those symbols and an altar is that place."

For many, the women's altar is itself a sign of religious immanence by virtue of its ancient emergence from the natural world. The very first altars, made of piles of stones or recognized in the circular pattern of trees in a grove, gave access to feminine earth-derived powers of growth, decay, and then growth

Pat Gargaetas's altar (detail) is covered with lesbian and feminist symbols reflecting her concern for what she calls "altaring consciousness."

again. Jean Mountaingrove reflects on making an altar out of the compost heap which for her came to represent the presence of Hecate, the Greek goddess of dream interpretation and decay, she who invites the new through the disintegration of the old: "My own altars are mostly made by nature rather than by human hands.... I love the vitality in nature, her sacred wildness.... Yes, all the earth is a sacred altar bearing the mysterious and incomprehensible gift of life. By making altars here, I create

more and more reminders of that sacred reality—so that I never forget. When we mark a place as sacred and keep responding to it reverently, we are reminding ourselves that the earth is sacred and that we, too, are sacred beings.... And if we assemble a crate, a cloth, a candle, and a stone, we are setting up a miniature of the earth—an archetype—to remind us of that deeper knowing that *all* of the earth is sacred."

Barbara Brown Millikan's altar surrounds her computer and includes an eclectic array of spiritual resources: a clay statue of the Goddess sculpted by her; a braided and wrapped piece of her hair; her wedding ring; and a Buddha. The central figure, seen between keyboard and monitor, is a carved Bear, her power animal.

Other women adopt the altar as a source of their own self-nurturance. Barbara Brown Millikan, a musician, emphasizes that, especially for women, the personal altar can be very much about finding and keeping an unperturbed connection with Spirit. It is "a place that is only mine and Spirit's, where I am accepted for exactly who I am.... Perhaps it is that we, the caretakers, must find a way to care for ourselves, honor ourselves and our Spirit connection as well." And, as lesbian-feminist Pat Gargaetas emphasizes, the altar is a place where, "a woman seizes power, the power inherent in symbols, the power of individual action to change the world beginning with herSelf."

As a mirror of self-reflection, growth, and change, the altar becomes a site where women claim and exercise an unencumbered sense of their own spiritual effectiveness. Sarah Johnson emphatically claims, "I relate to the deepest portions of my soul at my altar. The most primitive urgings and primal cravings. I don't censor, I just *am* in worship." The indwelling and individual character of relationship with the Divine is one of the central insights of home altars. Margot Adler, writer and Wiccan, declares: "All of these images are windows. And doorways. An altar is a collection of special objects that are doorways to your own soul and being. These images allow you to enter a deeper reality through gazing at them, through looking at them, through touching them, through being with them."

Whether providing access to external or internal aspects of the Divine, the home altar is known by the terms of a particular intimacy it emphasizes. At the very heart of altar-making is a woman's daily choice to engage the sacred on her own terms. Celeste West makes a crucial distinction: "I think the biggest tragedy is that the pulpit replaced the altar in the temples or churches. There is too much speaking, directing…intimacy has been taken away, the intimacy of being one's own spiritual guide. That's what can really happen at an altar." Sra. Gloria Rocha, a Texas-Mexican mother and homemaker, asserts the value of such intimacy in defining her bedroom altar dedicated to the Virgin of San Juan, a Mexican-based aspect of the Virgin Mary: "Everything here. I put it here. All these things are mine. For me and, yes, for Her. You don't feel good when you don't have all this. Is like you need to eat, I need to have that. I have that. I pray every day.… I sit down with Her and I pray my prayers. It's like I have a small little church.… I don't need to go to church to feel close to God or Mother of God. That—it don't mean nothing.…" Sisters Elvira and Hortensia Colorado, too, emphasize the daily presence of the altar in their lives: "Spiritual is not the same as religion, spiritual is part of daily life. That's what an altar is all about. It's not separate. It's part of what you do every day like getting up, washing, eating. It's part of daily business." The altar feeds a woman's spiritual hunger; Sra. Petra Castorena calls her altar "my source of nourishment," and Voodoo priestess Miriam Chamani echoes this when she says, "The altar is a focus. A center. It's like when you're looking for something, you find it there. The altar is the plate, the dish. We can all feast off that force.…"

Unlike the altars in the church or temple which have a certain stability and rigidity framed by dogma, custom, and male exclusivity, women's home altars are rarely set; instead, they expand and change—items are added or subtracted—following their maker's personal and spiritual evolution. As artist Jan Gilbert finds, altars can be messy with the process of living: "My altar is a jumble as you can see, but it is a jumble of the process—every kind of lucky charm, everything decrepit—it's all here. This a source for me.… I can't go to an altar and kneel and pray. I move around it. I work in proximity to it. I look at it. I interact with it. I definitely appeal to it." The meaning of images on the altar is encountered, not fixed. Individual concerns mark each altar's purpose and construction, visibly representing a woman's own choices of what is to be

Petra Castorena's flower-strewn altar dominates her small bedroom in Laredo, Texas. Gesturing broadly, she proclaimed, "This is mine—my altar."

At her home in New Orleans, Miriam Chamani's temple room is filled with altars, each one inviting the presence of a different African-based *orisha*, or spirit-deity.

wished for, remembered, loved, and venerated. Most home altars are revealing visual "texts" of a woman's history. As writer Judith Gleason claims, altar-arranging is about "bringing found objects into subjectively satisfying relation.... The energy generated by these juxtaposed things, their latent poetry, far exceeds that of any putative autobiography.... Such an altar is a miniature world produced by reverie which...becomes a metaphorical representation of the Self."

The miniature world of the altar tells the story of its maker in terms of her relationships—to the Divine, to herself, and to others. Wiccan Kate Roman finds in her altar "a place where I can connect on a daily (hourly!) basis to the Goddess and God. It reminds me of who I am, what I am, of my place in the universe. It connects me to all those women (and men!) in the past who remembered Her, loved Her, and devoted their lives to Her. It makes me part of a living chain of love and remembrance." A visible sign of connection, the altar also provokes a woman's desire *for* connection. The multitude of images on Ursula Kavanagh's altar are touch points with the many friends who gave them to her: "Building my altar has been a slow and gradual process.... I keep objects and mementos of places I have been and friends and lovers I have known.... The response from my friends has been enormous; I now have over one hundred pieces on my altar." The images on Yemaya Wind's altar are "reminders" to give reverence to her relationships with family, friends, and the earth: "These little Chinese figures represent my son and daughter.... I have healing stones, crystals. Many things I value are gifts. This bear vertebra from Susan; this carved bead from Victoria; this piece of black asteroid from Betty. My bedroom altar is about healing and marriage. Here I have family portraits and activated crystals and flower essence."

The representation of relationship becomes the *creation* of relationship in ritual activity at the altar. Renee Dooley, who describes herself as an Afra-

Miriam Chamani's altar (detail) to Erzulie, the Afro-Atlantic goddess of love and beauty.

American-HoodooWitch-Artist-Woman, exemplifies the patterned way in which relationships with deities and ancestors are sustained through repeated acts of communication: "Here's what I do for my Ancestors each Sunday. I get up, make a pot of coffee, take the glasses from the *bovida* and fill them with fresh water. I give them new candles, flowers, food, coffee, and incense. There's a special prayer said to them.... In it I honor the Creatrix of the universe, the world, those initiated priest/esses who have passed on, blood relations and spirit guides, and ask for the blessing of the living priest/esses of the house. After this I thank the ancestors for those things they've helped me with the previous week."

Many women, such as Renee, have several altars, but they distinguish those used as touchstones of belief or memory, places of display that solely represent relationships, from those used to actively engage relationships with spiritual powers. Feminist Margallee James makes this distinction clear: "To me, there are two kinds of altars. There is the passive altar and the active altar. A passive altar is part of one's decor. The Deity is perhaps invoked and then never really focused upon again. An active altar involves periodic focus for meditation, prayer, or ritual. Items flow to it and from it. There is spiritual activity there."

The active altar comprises a language of materials, a way of speaking through objects and a setting for actual communication. Marione Thompson-Helland identifies her altar, "as a sort of cosmic telegraph or message center, so I can communicate with the deity of my choice, the universal mind…and any of my friends or family…. Or—myself." Marione points to the profoundly liberating aspect of the altar's power to communicate. The altar makes past, present, and future equally and interchangeably available according to a woman's needs of the moment. Defying the limits of linear progress—the thrust of time which leads inevitably to death and the absence of communication—the altar allows its user to move freely through time, a different sense of time, which Mary Daly has termed the "power of presence…a time breakthrough…a continuing process…. What it is, in fact, is women's *own* time. It is our *life-time*. It is whenever we are living out of our own sense of reality…living in a qualitative, organic time that escapes the measurements of the system."[1]

As well as a place for effecting transformative communication, the altar is also a place where such communication becomes effective. Perhaps the most important kind of spiritual activity accomplished at the personal altar is healing. Many women state as simply as Marlene Terwilliger that, "My altars are healing, in their use and in their creation." And Vicki Noble notes the efficacy of the altar as a site for healing: "Healing requires that you pick a spot…you have to have a focalizing point…. The altar is a place where we focus our prayers…. We're always asking for our children, our community, our world." Healing is an essential gift, given and received at the altar. There both self-restoration and the healing of others is asked for and accomplished. Chole Pescina's close relationship

Ursula Kavanagh has slowly built her altar over years of assembling objects and mementos from friends and lovers.

with her miraculous saints—especially San Antonio who is petitioned to find lost things—was called on by many to help them in times of need. Her altar was always bright with candles lighted on behalf of others: "Those large candles on my altar are ones that have been brought by others for my saints. I light the small ones and petition a favor for somebody. I go there to my altar and I say, 'For the good health of a friend...a godchild,' and they grant it to me." For Vicki and Chole, as for other women, the altar's healing potential is based on a woman's irreducible will to assume relationship with the Divine and to access the power of divine intercession to enhance her and others' experience of living and being. Ultimately, a woman uses her altar as an instrument of creation, making and re-making connections which facilitate the progress of life itself.

Women recognize that their altars resonate with generative and regenerative powers. There a commingling occurs between a woman's creativity and the Creative itself. As artist Erika Wanenmacher says, her altars are "an acknowledgment of the creative forces, that wondrous dance of asking, receiving, and thanking." The creative enfolds the aesthetic. That "wondrous dance" Erika speaks of takes place within the altar's visual field where the sacredness of creation and its life-enhancing potential are given shape and expression in material form. The altar is a made thing and a process of making. It is an intentional gathering of symbolic objects, each having their own purpose, but each combining with others to elicit a visually compelling whole. Like any art work, an altar is a product of choice and strategy, an attempt to transpose contradictory materials through arrangement, embellishment, and so on, in the endeavor to create meaning. Author Suzi Gablik identifies her altar as "an expression of noble wild prospects for the soul, as an expression of the way we arrange things.... Altars are a way of orchestrating passion and articulating acts of perception entered into with the whole being.... Altars are a complete aesthetic environment that caters to all the senses." Rabbi Lynn Gottlieb compares the art of the altar to that of the narrative, saying: "To me the altar parallels a story in that a story creates a narrative which goes straight to the heart and has the power to invoke and evoke great archetypes.... I think an altar does this on a

Erika Wanenmacher's *In Case We Have to Leave* (1990) is a portable altar containing remembrances of life on earth—photos, plants—in the event that humans evolve off the planet.

visual level…. You know, we need it. We are sensate humans. If you want to have religious experience you need the aesthetic experience…the visual bond evokes the spirit."

Evocation is the primary aesthetic function of the home altar. Beyond what or who they represent in the sense of "standing for," the main purpose of altar images is to provide sources of vital engagement and exchange with powers known and unknown, seen and unseen. As Lynda Sexson suggests, the coming-together of art and religion never produces mere objects, but creates "the interplay between self and universe, whereby the self originates poetic participation in the universe, and the universe is formed by that information."[2]

Women validate this sense that the altar and its aesthetic scheme contribute to their "poetic participation in the universe." When I first met Sra. Aurora Treviño in Laredo in 1985, she showed me a carefully composed altar in the living room. There she had hung a print of Our Lady of Guadalupe. On a doily-covered shelf below it she placed two flower-filled trumpet vases on either side of a statue of the Virgin of San Juan. The altar was simple but elegant in its symmetry, and she told me it was there because she liked "to show people who come into the house that I believe in the Virgins." This altar publicly displayed her faith to others. But before too long she said, "I want to show you something." Taking me through the kitchen to a back hallway, Sra. Treviño pointed to a tall shelf filled with a mix of saints' statues, holy cards, candles, pictures of her children and her parents, jars of buttons and pencils, trails of ribbons, drawings done by her grandchildren, collections of stones and shells, calendars, Mother's Day and birthday cards, bits of crochet, doilies, and other things. Turning to me she said, smiling: "This is my real altar. I know it's a mess. But I have everything here. All the things that give me a feeling of closeness to God, and the Virgin and my family. This is where I come to pray every day. Every day I come back here in the morning when no one is home. And I say my little prayers or I just sit here and think. My husband is always after me to clean it up and throw things away. But I don't.

Aurora Treviño calls her altar "my place." Located in a back hallway, it is filled with the autobiographical, idiosyncratic things that reflect the ongoing process of her life.

This is *my place*. Oh, it's a mess, but I just keep adding things. And it makes me feel good to be here."

Sra. Treviño's assessment of her two altars reveals the critical distinction women make between merely representational objects and those that clearly engage the active imagination—memories, feelings, and responses—of the altar-maker in her own creation of an aesthetic union between the sacred and the mundane. Sra. Treviño's reflections on her "other" altar invite further consideration of the religious and aesthetic tradition that has led so many women to make their own sacred space: "my place."

CHAPTER TWO

A Mexican-American
mother photographed with
her child in front of her altar
in South Texas around
1940. Immigration has
brought diverse women's
altar traditions to the United
States over the past two
hundred years or more.

MATERNAL LEGACIES

inheriting the altar tradition

Many women's altar traditions of different ethnic and cultural origin are continued by immigrant and diasporic communities in the United States. From their native lands—and often at great personal sacrifice—women from Cuba, Haiti, Mexico, Ecuador, Guatemala, Puerto Rico, Thailand, Vietnam, India, China, Italy, Ireland, Poland, Hungary, Greece, Russia, and other countries have carried with them the making of their altars. Leaving other precious things behind, they nonetheless brought their statues of Our Lady of Guadalupe, Durga, Kuan Yin, and Yemayá, their photos of family and friends, their curative potions and amulets.

Within the context of major historical religions, which severely limit or prohibit women's participation in public religious performance, women's beliefs have been fulfilled for centuries in personal and family practices. For many traditional Roman Catholic, Greek Orthodox, Hindu, and Buddhist adherents the home altar is a maternal legacy passed down the female line from generation to generation. In places as different as Mexican San Antonio, Japanese Los Angeles, and Haitian Brooklyn, women like Bereniece Alvarado, Nagi Hashiba, and "Mama Lola" keep their altars in ways learned from their mothers and grandmothers.

This legacy is deeply cherished. A mother brings her daughter into relationship with the same divine beings who have aided her, protected her, and shared

The ancient legacy of Eastern European, Russian and Ukrainian domestic altar traditions is apparent in the altar of Marie Paluch, a woman of Ukrainian descent who lived in New Jersey.

her joys and sorrows. She envelops her daughter in these relationships, and makes her comfortable with, and reliant upon, their representation in images on the altar. Rituals are taught, and sacred statues and pictures are handed down as precious gifts, often given on the occasion of a daughter's wedding so that she can set up an altar in her new home. Together mother and daughter maintain active relationships with the deities and ancestors who are their special allies in the everyday but highly important tasks of preserving relationships at home: caring for the family, solidifying networks of extended kin and community, and assuming the privileges and duties that attend every one of life's passages, from birth to death. Central to this "work of kinship" is the home altar where earthly and heavenly families are drawn together in images and rituals that prove their interdependence.

In no religion does personal devotional practice—the hallmark of the home altar—necessitate a priest or other male authority. Within traditional communities throughout the world women uphold a matrifocal legacy of religious custom. Family and community networks of women form an active religious base that, in a reversal of patriarchal hegemony, actually makes men dependent on women for divine intercession in insuring the prosperity and protection of the family.

Ancestral portraits uniting earthly with heavenly "kin" are evidence of the pride taken in the home altar as a repository of family legacy. This photograph, found in a "flea market" and dating from the 1920s–30s, is possibly of a Catholic French or Slavic altar from the New York area.

The home altar's broadest base in the United States is Roman Catholic, and includes various ethnic and national expressions. All the Catholic altar traditions that I have encountered, including Mexican, Italian, Irish, French, Czech, and Polish, are mother-centered. In meeting after meeting during the ten-year span of my work documenting Mexican-American and Sicilian-American home altars in Texas, women recounted their matrilineal religious legacy as it was reflected in their altars. Sra. Romualda Perez, whose mother Cipriana kept an exact replica of

LEFT Heirloom statues of holy figures are passed down from mother to daughter. Sra. Antonia Andrade holds figures of the Infant Jesus and the Virgin which belonged to her grandmother.

BELOW Matriarch Florentina Trujillo, whose home in San Antonio, Texas visibly overflowed with her devotion, taught the altar-making tradition to three generations of women in her family.

her mother's altar in the entryway to her home, itemized the things on her altar and proudly concluded, "Part is my grandmother, part is my mother, and part is from my sister-in-law."

Within moments of meeting her, Chelo Gonzalez took me to her altar, which features a flower-engulfed image of the sacred Mother of all Mexicans, Our Lady of Guadalupe. Eagerly she told me of what she called "the inheritance" she had received from her mother: "This Guadalupe was given to me by my mother, Maria Luisa Cruz, shortly before she died. She gave it to me because I was the eldest daughter.... Forty years She has been with me. My mother had great faith in Our Lady of Guadalupe. And from her I learned to love the Virgin and to depend upon Her for guidance and help in time of need. I learned from her the splendid beauty of Our Lady. The mother is the one who shapes the values of her children.... Just as my mother did, I bring my children here to pray with me. I have seven boys and one girl, named after my mother. I will give her the Virgin so that she may have an altar."

Sra. Vencesuela "Lala" Treviño's keeps a prominently displayed altar in her living room, and when I asked her why, she silently motioned me to follow her into the bedroom. On a chest-of-drawers stood a hand-carved mahogany niche containing very old images of Our Lady of Guadalupe and the Virgin of San Juan. A candle flickered in front of this altar which had belonged to Sra. Treviño's mother: "Before she died she gave me the charge to keep a candle lighted for the Virgin.... She left me that charge and I will take it on until I die.... She had a

OPPOSITE ABOVE As the eldest daughter, Consuelo "Chelo" Gonzalez inherited her mother's image of Our Lady of Guadalupe, on the right. Eventually, Chelo will give the image to her daughter.

OPPOSITE BELOW Early in life, many Mexican-American girls are taught by their mothers to rely on the protection and guidance of Our Lady of Guadalupe.

Standing at an intersection between the major rooms in her home, Romualda Perez's tall, narrow altar (detail shown) holds objects given to her by her mother, her daughters, and her husband's family.

The St. Joseph's Day tradition is celebrated in Gloucester, Mass. by women like Mrs. Margaret Giacolone, a member of The Mother of Grace, an association of fishermen's wives and mothers who present altars in thanks for divine protection from the dangers of the sea.

devotion to the Virgin of Guadalupe and the Virgin of San Juan.... She had the tradition of having the candles and, me too, since she left it to me." When I met Sra. Treviño in 1985, her mother had been dead for twenty-seven years.

Besides her everyday altar, Sally Cantarella practices a Sicilian altar-making custom, centuries old, for St. Joseph's feast day on 19 March. St Joseph's altars are filled with food—cakes, cookies, decorated breads—in an excessive display of gratitude. With the help of female relations and friends, a woman gives an altar in thanks for a particular miracle—recovering from illness, finding a job, giving birth to a healthy baby—granted to her by St. Joseph.

As Mrs. Cantarella explains, this is a maternal tradition that affirms the care a woman shows for the welfare of her family, friends, and community: "It's such a beautiful devotion, really.... I learned [it] from my grandmother. When you live with someone, they sort of tell it to you all the time. Grandmother had an altar every time one of her four boys came back from the service." At the top of the St. Joseph's Day altar, an array of holy statues and images records the devotional history of its maker. In addition to central images of St. Joseph and Mary, Mrs. Cantarella's altar held statues of St. Peregrine, patron of those ill with cancer; St. Jude, patron of impossible causes; St. Michael, protector against crime; and many others. "All the saints

on my altar, they're the ones I've prayed to all my life…the Guardian Angel— I have her because my daughter was coming home one day and it could have been a terrible accident…. I said, 'The Guardian Angel must have put her arm around her,' and I said, 'I have to honor her,' because I feel like the Guardian Angel really had put her arms around her. Then the Holy Family is who I prayed to help my husband Joe, to keep him healthy and strong to fulfill his obligations of everyday living. And St. Teresa I also—in my younger days—prayed to for special favors. And the Infant Jesus of Prague was Katherine's, my partner's. We had a dress shop together, and then she died of cancer. This was her statue. I told her…'Katherine, don't you worry.' And she said, 'I won't be here for your altar….' And I said, 'That's something we don't know…. But I will promise you if you're not with us, your Infant Jesus will be on my altar.' …Then there's all the food. But you have so much help…. The women come for nine days and cook and make the cookies and arrange everything. I just supervise. Different ones will make different donations of time, food, and money. It just all goes together…. It's really a great tradition…. It's a lot of work. But some things are worth it."

While in name dedicated to St. Joseph, the patriarch of the Holy Family, in fact this altar tradition openly celebrates maternal and domestic legacies, values and practices. The subversive impulse in all women's altar traditions is played out in the excess of this one, which dramatically weds religious belief to an ideology of reproduction. All the labors of this feast are symbolically invested in promoting the value of women's kin work, support, and care. In other words, it is through the care and nurturing shown to St. Joseph and the Holy Family on this day that the importance of a woman's daily care for her earthly family and community is also made sacred. Pamela Quaggiotto, who has studied St. Joseph's altars in Sicily, argues that this sacralization further marks "women's role in creating life, in bringing new members into the species and recruiting new members into the family; it refers to the processes of change, growth, and progress of human life, which are made possible by women."[1] The St. Joseph's Day tradition richly demonstrates the way maternal legacies of the home altar express women's different understanding of their identity and power—as women and as mothers. The St. Joseph's altar is an elaborate "social construction" that proclaims a woman's "essential" difference. This is not to say that her biology is her destiny, but to affirm that her reproductive and regenerative capacities are vitally linked to her sense of being.

The historical depth of mother-centered concerns in the domestic altar tradition is further exemplified in the Greek Orthodox *eikonostasio,* the home site where sacred icons are displayed. Pre-dating Roman Catholic altar traditions, the *eikonostasio* has its roots in the hearth altar of ancient Greece. Brooklyn resident Angelike Manolakis set up her first *eikonostasio* some seventy years ago and maintained it until she died. There she extended the meaning of family to include various saints whom she referred to as her "companions." One of these was St. Paraskevi, to whom Mrs. Manolakis appealed for help with her glaucoma: "Every morning and every night I take her, hold her in front of my face, and make with her the sign of the cross on my eyes. She is my companion—and my eyes." Likewise, Calliope Phoutrides kept her *eikonostasio* in her home in Oregon, until her death. Born in the shadow of the Acropolis and named after one of the nine Muses, Mrs. Phoutrides came to the USA at the age of twelve. She was known for her ability to make *stefana*—the traditional crowns worn by bride and groom on their wedding day, and then kept on the *eikonostasio* as signs of the marriage sacrament. "We keep the traditions. [That is] the most important thing to pass on to children and grandchildren.... I never gave up because I had faith. I never said 'why' because I knew things. I think Mother taught me that."

A residual expression of the domestic altar, never routed by the Reformation, is the remarkable *Herrgottswinkle,* or "God's corner," found in Pennsylvania German Protestantism and throughout Germany as well, even in Protestant regions.[2] Folklorist Yvonne Milspaw's grandmother, who was a staunch Methodist in faith and Pennsylvania Dutch in heritage, kept a version of the *Herrgottswinkle,* which even included a number of Catholic items given to her by a friend: "In the corner of my grandmother's bedroom, right by the closet, there was a narrow shelf. About eighteen inches long and a few inches wide, it held a variety of religious objects.... Grandmother prayed for almost an hour each night...at her bedside where she could look up and see her shelf of sacred objects. At her death, her Memory Book contained a list of more than a hundred names of friends and relatives for whom she prayed every single night." The tenacity of an altar tradition among Protestant women, whose religion effectively prohibits the personal use of images, is provocative in its implications; women have retained the tradition for their own reasons.

Personal altars related to traditional Buddhism and Hinduism are maintained in the United States by women of Asian heritage—Indian, Chinese, Japanese, Korean, Cambodian, and Vietnamese, among others. I have few examples from my own research, but these altar traditions are widespread and are beginning to receive documentation by others.[3] One type of Hindu home altar is called a *mandir,* or God's House. In Pakistani and Indian homes in the United States it is the site of women's daily and seasonal rites, including specific rituals which secure the long life of one's husband, the happy marriage of a daughter, or the general welfare of children. Women also maintain personal and highly cherished relationships with specific deities to whom they appeal for guidance and aid. A favorite is Durga, one of the ancient mother deities of Hinduism, who later became a warrior-goddess, and now combines her maternal and militant attributes in her function as family protector. Her festival season is celebrated widely by women, such as

In early autumn, together with her daughter and mother-in-law, Jayanthi Raman creates an altar dedicated to Durga, the Hindu goddess of courage and protection.

Jayanthi Raman, who came from Madras to Oregon in 1989. Together with her daughter and mother-in-law she creates an elaborate altar to Durga in the autumn.

In Japanese Buddhist homes, the altar legacy is ancestral in purpose. Sustaining a living connection with the dead is part of a woman's regular religious practice. At an altar called an *obutsudan,* often cabinet-like in construction, a woman learns from her mother to honor the memory of the deceased, principally her husband's relations. For her entire married life Nagi Hashiba has fulfilled devotion on her husband's behalf, regularly making offerings of rice, tea, and flowers to his kin, but she has also established a separate altar of her own: "We use the *obutsudan* to honor my husband's family. But I have an altar for my mother's picture in another room where I place flowers and rice, and talk to her picture." After speaking momentarily of the danger of earthquakes in California, she suddenly said to me: "You know, when the Big One comes, I know exactly what I'm going to do. I'll go over to my altar. I'll sit there and be with my mother and let everything crash in around me. And I won't be afraid. I'll go with her. We'll be together." Expanding an ancient tradition for her own purposes, Mrs. Hashiba exemplifies the profound degree to which women assert a connection to their mothers through altar-making.

On the African continent, women's private altars are widely associated with various fertility and mother goddesses. In the New World, African belief systems from Yoruba and Kongo were maintained during slavery, though altered, often subversively, to absorb elements of Catholicism. Emergent Afro-Atlantic religious cultures in the Caribbean, Brazil, and the United States came to reflect a vital hybridization. Current Afro-Atlantic altar traditions in the United States are found in a wide range of practices, each with its own history and point of origin—Haitian Vodou, Cuban Santería, Brazilian Macumba and Candomblé and Trinidadian Shangó. These religions, like their African counterparts, are based on a reverence for ancestors and deified personifications of natural forces and elements—water, thunder, and iron—called *orisha* (in Haitian Vodou, *lwa*). The *orisha* and *lwa* are worshiped and appealed to as spirit deities—Ezili Freda, Yemayá, Ogún, and Shangó, for example—some of whom have their Catholic counterparts. Oshun, the goddess of love, is associated with Mary, and Shangó, the thunder god, parallels St. Barbara, whose legendary murderers were killed by lightning.

Altar traditions within Afro-Atlantic religions are varied and complex. They incorporate images of Catholic saints, African ceramic vessels, Native American elements, crowns, coins, nails, draperies, medicines, and amulets. There are ancestral, spirit, and conjuring altars, but the most important is made to honor and house a deity who has chosen to live with—and within— an initiate, whether female or male. In Haitian Vodou, the moment of being possessed and owned by a god or goddess is referred to as "mounting" and this incurs a life-long bond similar to a marriage.

Religious scholar Karen Brown has studied for many years with Alourdes "Mama Lola" Macena Margaux Kowalski, a Brooklyn-based Haitian-American priestess who "replaced" her mother, Philomise, in the traditional role of serving the *lwa*. In turn, Alourdes is currently assisted by her daughter

Mama Lola, a Brooklyn-based Haitian-American *manbo* (Vodou priestess), seated in her altar room, 1994.

Maggie. Karen Brown concludes that while Vodou practice in rural Haiti has conventionally been consolidated in male hegemony, women's role in the religion thrives in the face of change. The shifting circumstances and blendings of urban and immigrant life have proved fertile ground for women's assumption of roles previously denied to them: "Generally speaking, the issue is flexibility. The ethos within a woman's temple is like that inside the home, where the mother moves in and out of her role as an authority figure as the situation demands...." [4] Alourdes attends her relationships with various *lwa* in a small, specially dedicated basement-room filled with altars.

Brown asked Alourdes about the origin of her first altar: "At ten years of age I had a spirit 'mount' me. I was a little child. My mother made a *pwomes* [promise]. She gave the spirit food, and then she said, 'No, Alourdes is too little.' And the spirit did not come again. Then I got married, I had children. The spirit come and mount me again and speak with my mother in her sleep.... When I *kouche* [got initiated], they give me my altar.... My mother show me how to do good, never do bad in your life.... I remember every single thing she tell me, because that's in my family! My great-grandmother serve spirit, and my grandmother, then my mother, then me." By inheriting the images and implements of her mother's altar, Alourdes received her mother's relationships with various *lwa* and the injunction to continue gifting them and receiving their gifts in the healing of others. The spirit who visited Alourdes to convey the message that she would inherit her mother's practice was none other than Ezili Dantò, the foremost Mother goddess in the Vodou pantheon, who is most often represented as the Polish Black Madonna, Our Lady of Czestochowa. In describing her to Karen, Mama Lola said, "*Lwa* Dantò is an Ezili, a black woman. She has two scars on her face..... When I see her in my sleep, she is always a beautiful black woman. She is a *lwa* who is very tough too.... A spirit who is hard. But she is a good *lwa*...she is!"

Certainly not every altar-maker claims a maternal legacy, but, as these examples from distinct cultures show, at the oldest, the most primary level, keeping an altar at home serves the integration of religious and maternal practices. In generation after generation, the domestic altar has served as the tangible inheritance of a woman's relationship—past, present and future—to her matrilineage. Being a mother does not simply constitute a biological fact or a social role; rather, motherhood is a sacred office of relationship. It is the ground of connection to all others. One day Chole Pescina told me her view of motherhood: "The woman is valuable. Very valuable. That's why Jesus cried [from the cross], 'Dios, Madre' [God, my Mother]. Mother is a very sublime word. He didn't say 'Dios, Padre' [God, my Father]." Taking liberties with Biblical authority to make her point, Chole asserted her understanding that mothers own the fundamental power of relationship. At the home altar Catholicism's Holy Mother is freed from the canonical bonds that place Her under the male authority of God and Christ. Her maternal authority is acclaimed by women such as Chole who understand that She is central to their concerns in giving and sustaining life.

Shamaan Ochaum, who is not a birth mother herself, still reveres the maternal impetus that drives the altar tradition: "I think women for good reason are the keepers of family history, the keepers of cultural tradition. Women are the keepers of the hearth. In so many...cultures women are the keepers of that culture's spiritual and genealogical experience.... Now this is not always true, but...by and large the survival of the species depends on women's sensitivity,...a maternal sensitivity.... The infant can't otherwise survive...the infant is the soul of the family, the soul of the culture. The infant is most precious and vulnerable. The woman is the caretaker of that and the altar is that physical place where the caretaking is done. For that soul. For the soul of the culture." Through making and tending their altars, women receive the benefits of a sacred validation of mothering. The discourse of the mother is a discourse of affiliation and attachment, of birth and rebirth. The home altar visually proclaims the importance of this discourse and is a medium for articulating its power.

The maternal roots in altar-making run deep. Altars embed the elemental forces that long ago came to be associated with reproduction and mothering. The most ancient domestic altars dedicated by women were seen as places for receiving and appealing to earth, water, or moon-derived powers of creation, fertility, and birth. Miriam Chamani explains the potency of such analogy with regard to water and the moon: "The mother always comes back.... The mother-force is the essence of creation. Water—the female—was the first altar. That is where spirit was first carried. Water is the womb of the universe. Water is the place to be. Woman's role was, from the beginning, always bringing light. A woman always knows better in prayer. She can always bring the prayer to rise. Now male/female balance is important. But each has a time. The moon is the quiet force. Woman is the quiet force, the moon force."

Laurie Lipton's drawing *The Life and Death of Mrs. Doll* (1994) reflects the artist's appreciation of medieval European triptych altarpieces, which opened to show the story of the nativity and other sacred narratives. This is the story of Mrs. Doll, based on Lipton's life with her mother, whom she nicknamed in real life, "Mommy Doll."

Many women remark that the first altar, and still the most important one to them, is Mother Earth herself. Hortensia and Elvira Colorado suggest that the earth, the woman, the womb, and the altar are analogous and inseparable: "The altar is very connected to women because the altar is like a womb; it's part of the mother earth—it's where we come from, from the womb of our mother, and from the womb of our earth mother and we go back to the womb of our mother, the earth…it's a circle and there is no separation; it's all connected; it's all one."

In paying homage to their natal mothers or to the Great Mother, the Goddess, artists create altars that reclaim a primal connection to maternal resources, or that celebrate the mother-daughter bond. In Laurie Lipton's elaborately detailed drawing in the form of an altar/house, each floor of the "house" records a phase in her relationship with her mother. Mexican-born artist Susan Plum recovers Ix Chel, the Maya Goddess of the moon, childbirth, motherhood, healing, and weaving in a series of altars dedicated to her different aspects. In pre-Conquest Mexico, Ix Chel was enshrined at

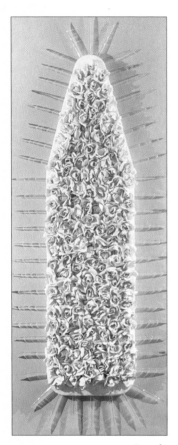

Susan Plum's *Ix Hun Ahau* (1992), one of a series of altars she made on ironing boards and dedicated to Ix Chel, the Maya Moon Goddess of maternity and creativity.

home and petitioned by women as the fertile progenitor of all things female. Plum refigures and updates the domestic legacy of this Mother Goddess by creating altars to her on ironing boards. Dixie Friend Gay, another artist and herself a mother, has created a large installation recalling the Triple Goddess— eight-foot-tall (almost three meters high) figures of the Virgin, Mother, and Crone surround a box containing a live boa constrictor. "The Protestant upbringing I had was always about the Trinity. Father, Son and Holy Ghost.... I wanted to work with a different idea of the Trinity—the Triple Goddess, the innocence, the fertile, the death mode..., it was a way to...acknowledge the sacredness of matriarchal religion. At the center was the box with a snake in it, symbol of the Goddess.... Her religion didn't die; it just...regenerated. It...shed its skin and was born anew.... It never died."

Reinvented altars dedicated to the Great Mother give visible shape to a feminist reappraisal of maternity. This also leads to a deeper appreciation of the remarkable tenacity of the domestic altar tradition as kept by mothers of different cultures and religions throughout the world. Under patriarchy, the feminine signifies reproduction and is considered limited by that capacity. Biological maternity is rendered powerless in the face of social paternity, and the social paternity bias strengthens the notion that women are the mere *objects* of maternity, not its *subjects*. But where women inherit from each other, and control symbols and metaphors of female reproduction, there is the possibility of rendering them positively and powerfully. As anthropologist Annette Weiner postulates, patriarchy can be viewed as the domination of women, but patriarchy may also be viewed as a failure to completely control women's reproductive and regenerative capacities.[5] One way that women prove the value and necessity of maternal images, histories, and processes is found in their maintenance and performance of the home altar tradition, inherited from the mother and renewed by each daughter.

The maternally potent
Red Goddess is one of three
large altars dedicated to the
Maiden, Mother, and Crone
which were incorporated
into Dixie Friend Gay's
installation *Lair of the
Goddess* (1990).

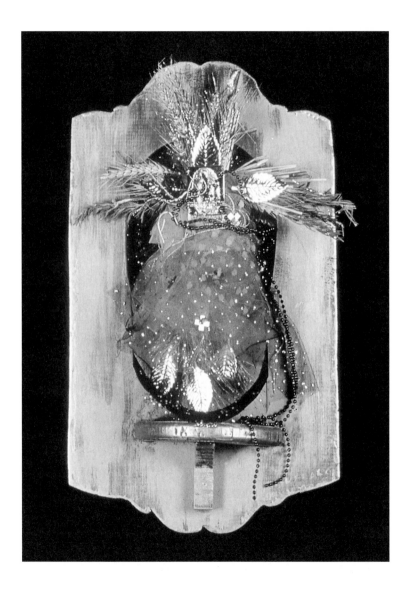

CHAPTER THREE

OTHER BEGINNINGS

new ways of coming to altar-making

In recent times women of different ages and backgrounds have come to altar-making through the enjoyment of a subjective and self-created religious reality. Many have consciously rejected patriarchal religions which they view as unyieldingly hostile to women. Their claim on the altar tradition is based not on religion *per se*, but on an intuitive or political—often a feminist—alignment with the *spiritual dimension*, a feeling for the sacred that is broadly based on individuality, receptivity, and creativity.

Spirituality is founded in devotion, the making of a personal vow, the dedication by choice to a source that holds the key to individual fulfillment. Devotion is bound to the body, to the emotions, to feeling, will, and desire, not to dogma. Spiritual devotion frames life in terms of experience and possibilities rather than absolutes; it engages the creative as a means of personal transformation. Altar-makers who come to the tradition in this way tend to view their practice as a source of self-empowerment that has nothing to do with given societal, religious, or family histories; it becomes, in fact, the very woman-centered means of overcoming the limits of these histories.

Many women speak of an attraction to the spiritual that was first expressed intuitively in collections of objects. Urban shaman Donna Henes suggests, "I think collections are beginning altars. The act of collecting may give you the beginning of a feeling about a spiritual issue. When you collect and select you begin accumulating memories and stories associated with the objects. They become your power objects associated with who you are." Collecting often begins in the childhood accumulation of potent objects, kept in special, sometimes secret, places. These "altars" take shape as resources for the imagination, as places set apart for inviting the magical. Rose Wognum Frances recalls the affecting quality of her teenage altar composed of moths' wings, pinecones, rocks, and other "objects I would find that somehow when they

OPPOSITE Rose Buffalo's *Rose Mystica* (1994) is from a series of her altars modelled after the "corn dolly" custom of annually making sacred fertility figures from the sheaves of harvest to insure future crops.

were put in a particular order, or relationship, or arrangement…it affected the feel in my room—made me feel present and fully there. It made something different happen…." Artist Nancy Blair remembers her dresser-top altar: "I've had altars since I was a girl…. I grew up in a trailer park, and my bedroom was no larger than 6' x 8' and that included a bed, a nightstand and my hallowed dresser at the foot of my bed. The top of my wooden dresser served as my first altar space, the place for my sacred girl's stuff. A white wooden jewelry box—a special eleventh-birthday gift from my mother—was the central focus on my girl altar. I cherished opening the small, gold-etched and framed front doors…. The moment I reached up to touch this special gift… I felt moved to sacred space…. When I opened my sacred jewelry box doors, I imagined that I was entering a fantasy land of dreams, treasures, and ancient wonders I couldn't possibly find in my trailer park world." Dixie Friend Gay made one of her first "altars" when she was eight: "I collected only rocks that had holes in them—kind of vaginal or breast-like. I didn't care what they looked like as long as they had holes in 'em, or clits, or nipples. Unfortunately, Mom threw those rocks away. She was a Christian fundamentalist…."

"Altars" such as these are indicative of the way, as children, women enter into heightened contact with material objects which signify an early desire for relationship between the self and what they later know to be the sacred. Nor do women lose their early connections to special things, particularly those found in the natural world. Angela King, director of an art gallery in New Orleans, has made several altars, and of a current one she says: "I pick up things that have significance to me: stones, bones, rocks. This sounds hokey because I'm such a city girl. But I do have these experiences with nature. I found a complete [set of] vertebrae—the whole spine of a deer—in the woods and I started wearing it…. I was completely taken over. I was reminded of where the power really is, where it really comes from. And it's not in consuming things or in my job…. It's in these profound moments in nature. I realized I had all these rocks I had collected since I was a teenager. I brought them together to make

Yemaya Wind's earth-healing altar is composed of dozens of crystals arranged to form a meditation mandala.

one altar of my rocks, bones, bark. That's about my connection to how truly powerful the earth is. The feminine power of the earth. That's what this is all about."

The feminist art critic Lucy Lippard suggests that these intuitively assembled nature-altars indicate the essential basis of art—and I would add women's spirituality—in a connection to earth, the *prima materia*, the life substance: "Art itself must have begun as nature—not as imitation of nature, nor as formalized representation of it, but simply as the perception of relationships between humans and the natural world.... Transformation of and communication through matter...is the rightful domain of all artists. Add to this the traditional, and ambivalent, connection between woman and nature, and there is a double bond for women...."[1] For many altar-makers the "ambivalence" of woman's relation to nature—her assignment by patriarchal decree to the "lesser" natural world and men's claim to the "superior" privileges of culture and society—is overcome by a newly awakened desire, spurred by feminism, to undo this false dichotomy. Feminist critics—among them Lippard, Susan Griffin, Suzi Gablik, and Carol Christ—disclaim the separation, and in its place reaffirm the crucially important cultural and religious connection between women and nature.

Altars are a profound expression of this connection. The oldest domestic examples made by women invited the beneficence of deified earth-power into the home. Bridging interior and exterior, altars are of the first order of cultural artifacts that utilize "transformation of and communication through matter," in Lippard's phrase, to signal and implement access between the social and the natural worlds. Altars are in essence thresholds between realms, and, as such, provide a place to resolve dichotomies. Many women now, as in the past, make altars to assert the interdependence between nature and culture and between the material and spiritual worlds. This assertion reifies the earth's natural powers of fertility, growth, and change that they may affect and improve social and cultural life. Recognition of the earth as the first altar—perhaps the only necessary one—is a founding principle of new traditions which revive altar-making as a sign of dedication to the earth's ultimate vitality. Over a ten-year period Yemaya Wind collected and was given dozens of crystals now made into an altar. She says that it is "about the energies of the earth.... I've set it up as a mandala—a round form to send healing back to the earth. It's a healing altar for the earth." For artists such as Donna Byars, Nancy Azara, Rose Buffalo, and Cherie Sampson, making altars from natural elements—earth and wood, animal skeletons, fur, and fire—not only recuperates woman's early history of sacred relationship to nature, but also affirms its lived reality today.

Of her large-scale altars made from trees, sculptor Nancy Azara comments: "In 1967 my daughter was born and I made a sculpture for her about the experience of her birth—carved from a very big maple tree that someone gave me. I started working with ideas about the tree and the self...the energy of the tree, listening to the tree, the spirit of the tree...the connection between women and trees."

Rose Buffalo, born on the Rosebud Indian Reservation in South Dakota, invokes the lineage of the Corn Mother in altars featuring stylized "corn dollies," based on the widespread custom of creating fertility figures out of corn or wheat to insure future harvests. Rose considers her "corn dollies" an expression of, "What I've chosen to be responsible for. What I see, hear, dream from the earth is translated into [these] figures. The Corn Dollies (Corn Mothers) are about the reverence I experience...[in] an organic and harmonious way of living with the earth...."

Taking responsibility for the earth in artistic acts of altar construction is an interactive process for artist Cherie Sampson, one that puts her directly in contact with the earth's cycles of growth, decay, and regeneration. Sampson has created numerous outdoor altars and sacred habitats using wood and other materials gathered on site: "Each piece reveals something of the character of the land where it was made and of my emotional and tactile perceptions of and interaction with it.... I began to utilize the materials, elements, and cycles of life and decay in nature 'herself', placing my body within the sculptural environment in a kind of living embodiment of *shakti*, the primal female generative 'fire'.... [My works allude] to female space (and the body, in general) and the 'myth(s) of eternal return': openings/enclosures, nests, holes, pathways, arches, serpentine ladders, and stairs. In a sense, my evolutionary path as an artist has taken me back through time—to the beginnings of art."

Many women have turned to earth-based and Goddess-oriented spirituality, particularly to Women's Spirituality, Wicca, Neo-Paganism, and revived Native American traditions, recognizing that their primary sense of the spiritual dimension is continuous with nature and the deities who represent principles of creativity, cyclic regeneration, nurturance, and healing. These newly emergent religious traditions, taught by women such as Starhawk, Zee Budapest, Shekhinah Mountainwater, and Diane Stein, began to take shape in the early 1970s, and ever since have continued to find an increasing audience of women. Personal altars made in these re-invented traditions reflect a serious commitment to overcoming patri-archal constraints with a new reverence for nature and the feminine Divine. Margot Adler explains that: "…the whole point of earth-based spiritual traditions like Wicca is that there is no dichotomy between the material and the spiritual world…the whole sub-versive character of this tradition is based in the idea that the material world is the ground of the sacred…the Holy exists in nature, in your mind, in your body, in your sexuality. All the dichotomies handed to us by patri-archy are false…. When we pluck the living flowers, what are they? They are spirituality without religion, without

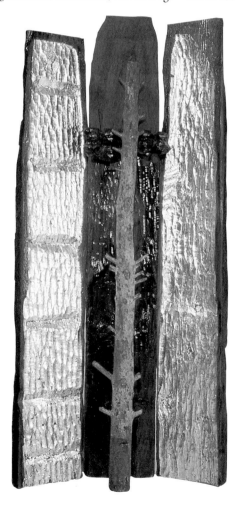

Carved, painted red, and radiantly gold-leafed, Nancy Azara's triptych-like *Tree Altar* (1994) evokes the sacred connection between women and trees.

ABOVE LEFT Cherie Sampson creates outdoor altars, such as *Fresh Water Fire Altar* (1992), made on-site with found materials and then used by her for solitary ritual performances.

ABOVE RIGHT Donna Byars has created many works, such as *The Snake, the Skull and the Pot* (1992–94), that synthesize aspects of ancient altars dedicated to animal spirits, earth forms, the Snake Goddess, and The Lady of the Beasts.

the church. The living flowers are our understanding of connection with all people, with all nature...."

Sabina Magliocco affirms that Wiccan, Dianic (the women-only witchcraft practice), and Neo-Pagan practices are not codified by restrictive dogma or a required set of rituals; rather, they are concerned with, "...a more meaningful moral order which includes feminism, respect for the earth, racial equality, cultural diversity, and an alternative to conspicuous consumption. The central ethical principle is, 'And it harm none, do what thou wilt.' " In Wicca, as in other traditions, altars are the vehicles of individual choice and creativity that help bring such moral claims to fruition.

Goddess Spirituality, often called Women's Spirituality, has been profoundly instrumental in acknowledging the immanent power of the feminine Divine. With a wide range of practitioners who take the source of their devotion from the long history of female deity traditions in many cultures, this spiritual reclamation makes use of the altar as a point of self-identification with the Goddess. Altar images of the Great Goddess, the Snake Goddess, Lakshmi, Hecate, Ishtar, Kali, Diana, and many others symbolically align women with gynocentric values affirming the legitimacy of women's beneficence, power, and self-determination, and the sacred difference of the female body and its life cycle. Heather Fox embraced the Goddess Aphrodite and discovered Her to be: "…the catalyst for very deep emotional and spiritual healing…because I grew up in a family where women were called whores, verbally abused, physically threatened, and generally treated with disrespect, and because I grew up with a religion that had no concept of deity as female…. The Goddess gave me a model for women being beautiful, powerful, gentle, strong, receptive, assertive, loving, and compassionate. The Goddess helped me to release the guilt and shame I felt about being a woman and to see myself as a beautiful and sacred Being." Two years after she came to the Goddess, Heather left a seventeen-year marriage to a man whose treatment of women was degrading. She reshaped her identity and sense of self-worth at her altar dedicated to Aphrodite. Newly conceived altars such as Heather's are contact points for a feminist understanding of the uncontained, unrestrained female self. Shelley Anderson's claim expresses what many have similarly said: "Without the feminist movement, and the encouragement that movement gave me to explore my feelings and express myself, I would never have made an altar. It's an act of power."

In her now classic essay "Why Women Need the Goddess" (1982), feminist theologian Carol Christ outlined the attraction of the Goddess for women, saying in part, "The affirmation of female power contained in the Goddess symbol has both psychological and political consequences. Psychologically, it means the defeat of the view engendered by patriarchy that women's power is inferior and dangerous. This new 'mood' of affirmation…leads to new 'motivations'; it supports and undergirds women's trust in their own power and the power of other women in family and society."[2] At their altars women depose the external authority of patriarchy by challenging it with an arrangement of symbols and ritual activities that name the internal authority

A lesbian-made altar from the early 1980s features a "butch" doll wearing a "Dyke" button.

of the altar-maker. A revival of the tradition among women today is very much about trading external for internal authority, using the private altar as a source of self-knowledge and self-blessing. Central to Nancy Worthen's altar is a porcelain mask of her face surrounded by "small objects from my present and past which...represent parts of myself.... I bring my conscious attention to this altar to remind me of who I am when I begin to forget.... I gather strength there to move out into the world. Or strength to separate myself from the world and remain alone."

Daphne LeSage began making altars when she "came out" as a lesbian: "Coming out brought me into a whole other way of looking at the physical world. It was about loving women and loving myself, loving my body and my image.... I've created this world of images here for me...making my feelings visible in space...." Lesbians have been at the forefront in treating the altar as a conscious source for enacting personal and political change. Among the acts of liberation that gave rise to the gay movement in the early 1970s was lesbians' claim to sacred space as necessary space for imagining the positive potential of their marginal status. If by definition patriarchy pushes all women to the margins of social importance, lesbians have been exiled to the farthest borders, even to the point of invisibility. But the fight to become present in the world has been fortified by a lesbian reversal of the stigma of marginality: it can be a chosen, even a desired position, enabling women to remain detached from the status quo. The lesbian altar then becomes a self-created center for venerating all that heterosexist patriarchy has attempted to deny or denounce: women's bodies, women's sexualities, women's heritage apart from men, and perhaps most important, as Pat Gargaetas observes, women's will: "In lesbian existence, how, and in what direction, a woman focuses her attention are philosophical, political, and spiritual choices.... Through altar-making...women willfully create value.... Altar work engages will in the making of value."

Lesbians, feminists, and Pagans have created new cultural and political ground for building the modern altar tradition. In all instances, new or revived altar traditions emphasize individual creativity, a true self-making of the relationship with the Divine. Intuition and imagination combine with eclectic religious knowledge; process is valued over product. The altar is never static; it evolves and changes, just as it invites the potential for personal change and transformation. Evelyn Hall Greiner's impulse to "build an altar" exemplifies this: "When I was twenty-four I knew the only way to truly commit to a spiritual path was to get sober.... About four months into sobriety, I was really struggling, and an inner voice said, 'It is time to build an altar.' I didn't really know anything about altars at the time.... I had never even really thought about them." Greiner found the first image for her altar at a thrift store: "I walked right over to this Mayan-looking Goddess. Her hands held a plate and it looked like she was blowing or singing into it. I picked her up and discovered she was an old Kahlua bottle—alcohol.... Perfect for my first altar dedicated to sobriety.... I still have her and love her twelve years later.... My altar...came to fill the void, the deep emptiness I felt.... It became my friend and guide.... This sacred place was and still is feeding my soul."

Women who convert to Western sects of Buddhism and Hinduism newly learn the age-old practices of devotion and meditation. Here the emphasis is on using the altar as a place for integrating self-understanding with the realization of ancient religious principles; the Buddhist concept of non-duality is one example. Celeste West, a Zen Buddhist, explains her use of the private altar: "Buddhist tradition is very iconoclastic. If you walked into my home and asked me, 'Where is my altar?' I would probably answer here [points to her heart]. In Buddhism the sacred experience comes from within; it's not from any outer being or creature—god or goddess or Buddha.... In Zen, everyone is Buddha, has Buddha-nature. In Buddhism we talk about 'the shining original face.' Everyone is born with the shining original face. All spiritual authority rests in you. Not only in you of course, but...there is not an Other; there is no dualism. It's not 'out there'—there is basically this inner being—everything is connected—it's all part of each other.... But in any tradition you need reification of beliefs and so we have altars.... There is the outer altar which shows something and the inner altar which is you. I need my outward altars to remind me of this."

All personal altar traditions allow tremendous latitude for experimentation with the meaning and use of images and symbols. In both custom-bound and newly active traditions, altar-making often results in an abundance of expression. Although there is usually one centrally kept altar used daily for devotion, many women keep multiple altars for different purposes. Relationship with the Divine is made more available and more specific by such dispersal. In Afro-Atlantic practice, for example, it is typical to maintain several altars to different *orisha*. Besides her central altar to Shangó, Aina Olomo keeps them for her Mother *orisha* Yemayá and for Oyá, the love goddess, among others. Mexican and other folk-Catholic domestic traditions often reflect an inspiring excess of religious display. Every corner of Bereniece Alvarado's house in San Antonio was filled with images of the Virgin and other saints, displayed with ceramic figurines, stuffed animals, and family pictures. Sra. Alvarado said, "You see Guadalupe all over my house. She's

Our Lady of Guadalupe oversees work done at the sewing-machine in this home in San Antonio, Texas.

always near me." But she distinguished this from her two other altars, one on her living-room mantle dedicated to Guadalupe's protection of her children, and one over her bed "where I talk to the Virgin every day."

Renee Dooley, who follows an eclectic spiritual devotion, catalogs her various altars: "I actually practice several different traditions which overlap in places. I am a Dianic Witch…and some altars reflect that tradition, and I also practice Hoodoo, which is the North American form of Afro-diasporic religion/magick, and I am a student of Santería, so other altars reflect the forms required for those religions." Susan Gray also keeps many altars, and she suggests that they form a continuum. The domestic environment becomes inclusive of all aspects of a woman's growing and changing spiritual motives: "At any given time I usually have two seasonal altars, a meditational altar, one that holds whatever spells I am working on, and one that holds recently gathered significant objects from travel and Goddess sites (holy water, soil, sand, stones, shells, feathers…). I also have two or three altars dedicated to different Goddesses whose energies or attributes I am trying to work with, and sometimes altars for special projects, as well as one for ancestors and animal spirit guides. I have altars in the house, my studio, and the garden. But in actual practice they are not as distinct from one another as describing them tends to sound. Objects may move from one to another over time, or purposes may mix and change."

A predilection for altars and religious ornament in their homes shows how remarkably pervasive daily association with the sacred is for many women. An image of our Lady of Guadalupe oversees work done at the sewing-machine or a picture of Artemis is taped to the refrigerator. The sacred embraces the quotidian in domestic space where women accommodate that meeting within the flow of everyday life. Author Caitlin Libera suggests that altar-making principles extend to general domestic design: "Table tops covered in family pictures, collections of stones and shells picked up on the beach, a 'we're having company' group of candlesticks, the 'my kids made these' corner of the refrigerator. All of these are shrines to memories, community, family, and are part of our shared experience, no matter how diverse we may be." In such special arrangements of commonplace things, women express more or less unintentionally what altars purposely propose: the efficacy of images and objects arranged as sources of identification and connection with others. Writer and artist Terry Wolverton simply claims, "Women have been doing it anyway. Somewhere along the line we began to call our activity *altar-making*, and, in turn, doing it more consciously."

In the 1970s, artists involved in the radically revisionist spirit of the growing Women's Art Movement defiantly elected to ignore the conventional distinction between "fine" art and women's "domestic" art. They discovered altar-making as part of a reinvigoration of the domestic sphere, reclaiming it as a determining frame for practices that inscribe women's creativity and subjectivity, not our passivity. As feminist art historian Arlene Raven explains, these artists came to: "*underline* the artistic nature of all forms of altar-making by women. The altar viewed as aesthetic model, performance genre, artistic object, and women's art—the very acknowledgment of the *existence* of the altar—begins to change our traditional white, male, Western-bound ideas concerning who the artist is, and how, and to what purpose, she creates."[3] Raven also says, "The altar, by definition of its form and use, is an artistic implement for getting and giving power. By acknowledging the legitimacy of the altar as a woman's art form we further legitimize and encourage a feminist understanding of art: that for us the assembly of images is not mere representation but a potent means towards realization of a new culture which both criticizes patriarchy and transforms it."[4]

Betye Saar, Mary Beth Edelson, Amalia Mesa-Bains, Nancy Fried, Jane Gilmor, and Rosemary Kelly are a few of the artists who first brought the women's altar into public settings for consideration of its history, aesthetic attributes, and political force; they continue in their altar work today. Mary Beth Edelson found the altar a perfect format for simultaneously reversing the patriarchal prohibition against women's spirituality and women's art: "What I was trying to do in those first altars was manipulate the idea that women could define spirituality in their own terms. I would take certain forms, such as the altar, that were very strongly associated with patriarchal religion, at least for most, and one thing I wanted to get across over and over again was that woman could be the primary sacred...being. In order to break through

The journey between worlds that the altar makes possible is emphasized in Betye Saar's transformation of a canoe into an altar in her installation *In Troubled Waters* (1993).

OPPOSITE ABOVE *Feline Birth-giving Goddess*, from Jane Gilmor's *Great Goddess: Çatal Hüyük Series* (1980) which incorporates images from shrines found at Çatal Hüyük.

OPPOSITE BELOW *Homenaje a Frida Kahlo* (1978) by Amalia Mesa-Bains, in collaboration with Carmen Lomas Garza and Rene Yañez was dedicated to the secular "goddess" of Chicana art.

those barriers...I had to capture the language—for example the language of the altar, its recognizability—and then have the nerve, the assumption, the presumption of putting it out with a totally feminist purpose." If the altar was assumed to be a patriarchal construction, Edelson unseated that assumption by reclaiming its origins in women's religious practice. In works such as *Great Goddess House Shrine* (1982), Jane Gilmor set ancient feminine symbols from Çatal Hüyük in a copper repoussé altar which enclosed a video of a ritual she performed. She suggested that the altar's first use as a sacred site for sculpted images of the Great Goddess could be reconfigured—resacralized—as a place for modern-day video images of the Goddess within herself.

In her altar work, Betye Saar's vocabulary of symbols reaches across time and space to invite an experience of multiculturalism as a source of access to the universal power of symbols: "....I refer to the sun and moon, or use objects collected in Haiti or Mexico—power from other countries. I'm drawn to ritual places all over the world—Europe, Africa, Mexico—where there are offerings of jewelry, personal items, relics—ritual places where things are accumulated.... My altar art is international, multicultural and religious. My altars become universal...." Saar freely appropriates distinct religious and ethnic symbols in an effort to mitigate separation. All her altars, the very first of which was *Mti* (1973), offer ways to journey between worlds. A recent work, *In Troubled Waters* (1993) emphasizes this most candidly: the altar is made from a blue-painted canoe emblazoned with cosmic symbols and filled with

up-reaching hands, universally symbolic of the human desire for contact with others. As Saar further says: "Curiosity about the unknown has no boundaries. Symbols, images, places, and cultures merge. Time slips away.... By shifting the point of view, an inner spirit is released, free to create." In their accumulation of diverse sacred objects and symbols and their daily practice of an eclectic range of rituals, many women have followed Saar in discovering the personal altar as a seat of creative spiritual choice.

Artists' approaches to the altar range from the universal to the particular. Chicana artist Amalia Mesa-Bains makes altars that refer specifically to her heritage: they define and elaborate the inter-sections between gender, race, and ethnicity in our society. Taking the Mexican Catholic home altar and Day of the Dead *ofrenda* as a basis, Mesa-Bains adopts traditional altar-making crafts (paper-flower making, for instance) and symbols (such as skulls, hearts, and images of the Virgin) to gain recognition for the beauty of folk religious and artistic practices she observes in her family and culture. In her capacity as curator of "Ceremony of Spirit" (1993), an exhibition that featured pan-Latino altar expressions in various

media, Mesa-Bains sought, as she does in her own altars, to define spirituality "as an ultimate act of resistance against cultural domination." Mesa-Bains creates altars as sites of "redemptive memory," repositories for cultural and familial history which assert what she calls "an ancestral imperative," and whereby, "memory becomes the instrument of redefinition in a politicizing spirituality." The home altar as an art of cultural memory and personal identity can be fused with a political, often a subversive, recognition of its ability to challenge hegemony. The altar absolves domination in its rich access to reverie and the residual; the altar defies by keeping, holding, and sustaining the means of familial, communal and cultural affiliation.

Like Mesa-Bains, the Afro-Canadian artist Jan Wade draws upon a rich heritage of altar and symbol traditions. Her visual imagery—the cross, the mermaid, the hands of the healer—incorporates the Afro-Atlantic religious symbols of Vodou and Santería, symbols that fuse "the sacred and the profane, Black and White culture, and pop art culture" into "a visual poetry of resistance." As a woman of mixed racial parentage, Wade adapts altar-making in what she calls "a fight against the plantation of the mind and the psychological effects of racism."

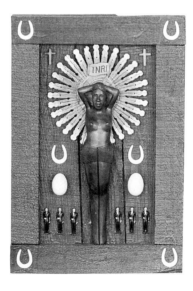

Jan Wade's *Soul Tone Poem-Ancestor Spirit* (1994), details shown here, exemplifies her politically charged combination of African-derived and pop-culture imagery in her altars.

So many women—artists, Wiccans, Goddess-devotees, and others—have recently chosen the altar tradition for themselves. But they are not unlike their foremothers who kept the tradition vitally alive before them. Making an altar is, and always has been, an act of women's intention. In whatever form it takes, the consciousness that gives the personal altar its particular significance is a woman's consciousness of what an assemblage of sacred, familial, natural, or secular items symbolically presents as her view of the spiritual world. The benefits of the altar practice come from a woman's own sense of intimacy with the sacred. She invents for herself the usefulness of symbolic objects, both sacred and secular, universal and personal, according to her own history, needs, desires, and beliefs. She makes a place for these objects; she sets them apart; and she assigns them their meaning and purpose.

CHAPTER FOUR

Rose Wognum Frances made an altar *Mr. Bear's Mantle* (1982) to house the coat she fabricated from silk, cobweb, leaf ghost, and dragonfly wing to be worn by Bear, the stuffed animal icon she inherited from her mother.

CREATING CONNECTIONS

altars and the desire for relationship

As much as women's personal altars reflect individual expression, their purpose, and ultimately their special worth, springs from a universal motive: the tradition is steeped in the symbols, values, and intentions of relationship. In making their altars, women assemble images that represent the power of and need for good relationships and positive affiliations. As a visual testimony to the emphasis that women place on creating links between people, between things, and between realms, the altar specifies a context for building and sustaining relationship. A center from which women can advocate their world view, the altar is both a model of and an instrument for relationship. It is a place for understanding the presence of the Other, certainly in the sense of knowing the Divine, but also in the ethical sense of connecting to otherness and others as a goal of human living. Artist and rancher Jeanne Norsworthy suggests that the need to connect is at the heart of women's spiritual aptitude: "Who knows why women are more spiritual than men. Men are about power, and women are about connecting.... Women deal with basic life and death issues as part of our gender.... Whenever another person and I connect on a level that is equal and emotionally truthful, that is a spiritual experience for me. Whenever I connect with nature, as an equal, and as "part-of," I have a spiritual experience. To me an altar is a tool that reminds me, prods me, provokes me to seek that connection...."

At the altar the desire for relationship breathes life into religious beliefs and practices that assert the prime importance of giving care to and receiving it from others. It is a site for seeking divine help in initiating, restoring, remembering, and protecting the vitality of human and natural relationships, and appeals made there catalog those lived situations that demand care or implicate the need for connection: healing the sick, asking for a blessed union in love or marriage, soliciting the healthy birth of a child, remembering the dead, sheltering loved ones from danger, praying for self-renewal, affirming the legacies of kinship and friendship, and seeking harmony with nature.

Altar-makers are all ultimately seeking affiliation. Of course, the first and generally most desired affiliation is with the Divine. As a point of intersection where the gap between the human and Divine is bridged through a process of intimate identification and exchange, the altar is a place of profound merger between Self and Other. Barbara Brown Millikan explains: "Altars demonstrate the value of connection; in any tradition, they symbolize the interaction of the Divine with the individual.... At the altar, Self and Other become one entity. The Self creates an object arrangement that becomes the Other, signifying the Divine Other who is also in the Self and in everything in Nature. Although the creation of an altar differentiates the two, its purpose is to remind the participant of the unification of God/dess, Nature, and Self. What you give to an altar,... you give to yourself and the Divine, and subsequently receive. Polarities melt here. In sacred space, parallel lines meet...." Millikan practices altar-making out of a Women's Spirituality tradition which she has defined and honed to her own self-understanding and need. She discovered her important relationship with the Native American Bear Spirit, whose sculpted image is placed centrally on her altar: "In finding Bear, I found a Spirit role-model for the kind of powerful woman I wanted to be, and the Mother who would raise, advise, teach, and honor me the way a powerful woman should be. Other power animals have joined her in talking with me, but she is my Mother. And she is the focus of my altar as well."

For many traditional altar-makers, identification with the Divine Mother is also the primary relationship. Maternal labors directly affecting positive relationships within the family are validated and assisted through intense affiliation with Mother deities. Gloria Rocha speaks of her alliance with the Virgin of San Juan, a manifestation of Mary, the Mother of God, whose image is a doll-like figure with copious black hair wearing a triangular-shaped blue dress and a large crown: "I keep Her here with me, here on my dresser and I pray and pray and pray to Her every day. Like I told my daughter, I say, 'I'm your mother right now, but you just remember I won't be here for the rest of your life. That way if you need a mother you can go and talk to Her after I leave.' …She's a mother and she knows the way a mother feels and suffers…. She help us be better mothers…. She help everybody. She is the Mother to everybody…. But…She knows how a mother feel and that's why I think we get more close to the Mother…to ask Her to help us…to raise the kids, because you know it's not easy to raise kids…. We, the mothers, we are more close to Her."

In Aina Olomo's African-based *orisha* tradition, a deity claims an individual after a year-long process of initiation. The initiate, whether male or female, is referred to as a "bride," and the new couple is "married" on the day they are given an altar—a place to inhabit the relationship. Aina's marriage to Shangó has been ongoing for thirty years: "Shangó is my main deity. He is the King. He is the Love of my life. We have a very complex relationship. He is my husband, my father, my best friend, my guide. He's it. He's it. For me personally, he's what gives me a joy for living. He's my passion…without Shangó I do nothing…. My relationship with him is completely intact."

Gloria Rocha maintains an active relationship with the Virgin of San Juan whose doll-like image dominates all others on her bedroom altar.

Affiliation with trans-historical deities and spirits is shown by their images and symbols on the altar, but usually these are framed within a profusion of items that represent a woman's own history of affiliations; women cover their altars with signs of their personal relationships. An autobiography, a personal narrative of meaningful connection with sacred beings, family, friends, animals, nature, and the self, is "written" in objects that accumulate and change over time. On Margarita Guerrero's folk Catholic altar, each picture of a saint or statue of the Virgin recorded not only a lifetime of relationship with those sacred beings but also with friends and family members who had given Sra. Guerrero these images. She surrounded them with decorative knick-knacks received from friends—a trio of ceramic birds, a glass orb enclosing dried flowers—and embellished the setting with ribbons saved from Christmas and birthday packages. From the least to the most significant object, Sra. Guerrero was able to recount the history of each item on her altar.

In her altar-making, lesbian-feminist Hawk Madrone discovered a place to recognize the importance of a self-determined connection with herself and others: "I was raised a Lutheran. I remember that the altar was something you didn't go to. It was removed. You didn't touch it. It was off-limits. The same in synagogue. The altar belonged to men. It had to be this thing cut off from you in order to make it special. Now, what my altar means to me is the complete opposite. It is about what I am most intimate with. Everything on my altar is something I put there, or a friend gave to me. Everything on it has an intimate meaning for me. For example my companion creatures…animals

Among other items on her altar which catalog her relationships, Hawk Madrone keeps the dog "necklaces" of animal companions who are no longer with her.

who I have been dear to, who have been dear to me. This necklace or Missy Moonshine's fur—she died in 1983—these are tokens. Their power is in what they call up in me. I recall who I was. Who they were. I have my grandmother's home-made Christmas decoration. She died when I was one and a half. But this [decoration] is a link to a maternal past…. I don't get along with my mother. I've had a difficult time with her. But once while she was here…she went down the road and picked up a rock and put it here. I've wanted to take it off the altar, but I can't. If I focus on it, I have to wrestle with it, but that's good…. I have these statues of Kuan Yin and the Virgin Mary and this altar cloth—a doily made by Bethroot's great aunt. I have this candlestick, it was one of a pair I gave to my sister. I gave her the pair and she returned one to me. I have this rock from her. Her love for me is a treasure in my life. When I bring my sister's rock to me, I bring her love."

Altar objects have a potent ability to recall relationships from the past and to affirm relationships in the present. Rose Wognum Frances created a special altar for Mr. Bear, a stuffed animal that she inherited from her mother. Mr. Bear is not only a touchstone of Rose's childhood, but is an important agent of connection and communication with her mother today: "When I was sent to boarding school my mother gave me Bear. And he was always with me.... He's my relationship with my mother. It's through him that we spoke and deeply connected by talking about him.... The Great Bear Mother, Ursa Major in the sky, has always meant everything to me.... More than my mother, she was the Great Mother. But Mr. Bear really was my communion with my mother.... Because my mother needs a mediator and I knew that.... She never hugged us or kissed us.... There was this other way. But it was wonderful. We can say a lot through the Bear. We still do. She'll call and we'll have a full conversation about what Bear is doing.... He is an archetypal image for me in every way. The Bear is with me—always."

Artist Laurie Zuckerman created an altar that records her relationship with her husband: "I gathered up a cache of natural objects, all of which have ties

Laurie Zuckerman's *Earth Goddess Altar* (1997) collects stones, shells, a crane's egg, a butterfly, and other gifts of nature; each is tied to significant moments in her relationship with her husband.

to our relationship. Mold-blotched gourds, which we had grown in our own earth, rocks we had picked off of desert floors.... Every item traced its route to a significant time in our life together. The first present Tom gave me—a shell off the beach in Costa Rica. The first Christmas present I gave Tom—an iridescent blue Morpho butterfly. Our two favorite wedding presents—a crane's egg nesting in a wooden bowl carved in the shape of a bird.... Presiding over the entirety, I placed the...goddess statue that I gave to Tom this past Christmas...."

The home altar is a consciously created site of heightened familiarity. It feeds in its keeper an emotional center around which clusters a constellation of trust, respect, love, and care. The emotion of connection is felt in the very typical placement of photographs of family and friends. Propped against a sacred image, weighted with a special rock, or seen in the light cast by votive candles, they demonstrate the relation the altar-maker assigns between her "earthly" family and the "heavenly" family. Gloria Rocha tucks snapshots of her children at the bottom of her statue of the Virgin of San Juan: "Sure, I keep the kids right here with me. When I'm praying to Mother of God I'm talking about them with Her. And I'm looking at Her and looking at them and She's looking at me and them, too."

Sharon Smith has created a houseful of altars, each a visual, tactile reminder

A kitchen altar made from an old cash register is one of many altars Sharon Smith has created throughout her home to remind her of the wealth of her friendships, near and far.

of her continuous connection to friends all over the world. "Everything in my house—all my altars are about friends.... These things on my altars are very good friends.... This is all about my sense of inter-connectedness.... People supporting me.... I'll look at something and say, 'My friend, I wonder how she's doing?'.... Some think it's odd—they think of it as materialistic in a negative sense—but to me it's Glorified Materialism."

The altar's "glorified materialism" invites a trans-formation; mere objects become intimate subjects in a pantheon that enjoys an easy correspondence between universal and personal symbols. Universal symbols—the statue of the Virgin or the votive candle—are subjectified within the jurisdiction of personal symbols—a lock of hair or a photograph of a friend—that signify a woman's individual identity. Simultaneously, a process of universalizing the intent of personal symbols makes them available not only as records of an altar-maker's life but as "affecting presences" that play their part in a woman's evolving creation of a spiritual relationship with the Divine, with others, and with herself.

Nowhere are the personal and the universal joined more poignantly than in the creation of the memorial altar which serves as a meeting place between the living and the dead. Women have always played a primary role in maintaining relationships with the dead; many cultures, both ancient and contemporary, assign birth and death, and the continuity between them, to a woman's ritual custody. Certain seasonal altar traditions including the Mexican *ofrenda* and the Wiccan Samhain are specifically dedicated to the memory and preservation of relationship with ancestors. But many women also use their daily altars as places of affiliation with the deceased. Artist Sheri Tornatore remembers her Italian grandmother's altar: "My grandmother's main devotion was to St. Teresa of the Little Flower. Her main altar was erected around her dead son Carmen—the oldest—who was killed in World War II. His picture was very big and very brown. He was in uniform. She had statues around it and she had pictures of her other kids there, too. And candles. I remember that as a devout place—right there on the TV."

Sra. Maria Perez's altar, dedicated to Our Lady of Guadalupe, is dominated by an old, hand-tinted, formal photograph of her parents set on the wall near the Virgin. The image of Guadalupe and the portrait occupy the same plane: "I like them looking at me. I like to look at them, all together. I say my prayers and I look at them. Or I just pass by and I see them." Ornately framed ancestral portraits or photographs often occupy a prominent position on or near home altars. Usually raised high, at the same level as images of tutelary deities, these heirlooms reflect the remembrance and respect which is given to forebears. Family history and sacred history are united at the altar site, bearing witness to a lasting heritage of relationships that binds kin together through time and in spite of it.

This long-lived memorial tradition spills over into creative contemporary practice. After the death of her beloved sister Barbara, Marlene Lortev Terwilliger turned to altar-making as a way of creating a visual narrative of the future they could continue to share together.

"It was the death of my sister that led to my first altar. Even as I was sitting *shiva* [the Jewish mourning rite] I knew that I could not return to 'normal' existence without finding a formal or ritual way of maintaining her presence in my life. I thought about a fantasy we'd shared...when we were old we'd live together in a little house by the sea.... I discovered a marvelous deck of Alice in Wonderland cards and out of them constructed our house. It was perfect:

Marlene Terwilliger created an altar *We Share the Moon* (1991) in remembrance of her deceased sister Barbara.

a story from our childhood, and a link to our father who'd been great at amusing us with his talent for building elaborate structures with cards.

"Once the house was built I decided we'd occupy it in the form of Matisse women, odalisques, who have always touched me and felt 'true' to us. I found a cafe table and chairs, coffee pot and cups.... I wanted a four-candle holder for the four seasons.... Finally I found the perfect one, adorned with mermaids.... It was only for three candles but that turned out fine because I found a separate holder that would be right for the candle of each season.... By then the shape and form of the altar were clear. I had a Lucite box made, then filled it with sand from the beach. I gathered pinecones, shells, stones, bought little objects I thought we'd have or would be there—a typewriter, writing pad and pencil, a fish, a bird.... I called the altar *We Share The Moon*, a translation of the Chinese characters on the card in the center of the altar. On the backside of the card there is a poem—'I look up at the moon/And my heart feels you/ Although a thousand miles away/Watching this same moon.'

"The altar is very 'alive' for me. It continues to evolve and change as I add new objects, things Barbara might have wanted to include in our world.... Recently I added a little altar within the altar, and a skeletal bone I found on the beach.

"...Each solstice and on my sister's birthday I perform a ritual. I buy fresh seasonal flowers, surround the altar with her pictures, change and light the candles, burn incense. I play music softly, meditate, speak to her, dance, or cry.... The altar is a memorial, a way of honoring my sister, of keeping her with me in my life...forever. It is a way to express my grief and my love."

Cristina Biaggi's memorial altar to her mother draws a connection between the Great Goddess and this beloved parent: "My altar...consists of my Mother's photo when she was twenty years old, a candle, which is constantly lit, fresh flowers, and several Goddess figurines and shells, surrounding my Mother's photo.... I sometimes pray to my Mother...and to the Great Goddess.... The Sleeping Priestess of Malta...is important to me at this point because she is portrayed in a 'dream incubation state'...she has helped me communicate with my Mother.... I have had several very nourishing and rich dreams about her."

Writer and scholar Joan Marler worked for many years with renowned archaeologist Marija Gimbutas, and since her death has been actively preserving her scholarly legacy. Marler's altar to Gimbutas invokes her mentor's presence: "I listen to Marija to direct the work. The altar is a place to channel and to receive the ancestors. It's a living form. They need us as much as we need them." As links between the living and the dead, memorial altars perform the task of upsetting the linear progress of mortal time; instead time shifts back and forth from present to past to future in immortal time. This fluidity is vested in communication. The altar, as Marler says, is a "living form." It defeats absence and separation with an impetus towards connection, even with those who are "gone."

Artist Kathy Vargas uses photographs to make altars that link her in imagistic "conversation" with loved ones—living and dead. For Kathy, the central purpose of an artist's altar work is communication and connection: "What's important when artists make altars is that they have a personal connecting point to that altar. You can make the most fabulous, incredible altar, but if there is no connecting point, it leaves us cold.... When an altar doesn't work, it's because the maker hasn't invested the personal...hasn't said, 'You've got your heart coming from here and here's my heart coming to meet you halfway.' The whole thing about that active intermediate space is that you've got to put yourself there. You can't just haul the Sacred down and look at it.... You've got to interact with the Sacred, tell it your problems, your joys. The reason I quit going to church is because that conversation wasn't happening for me there. And the reason I continue to...make photographs— that are in fact for me, altars—is because that interaction, that conversation is happening there."

Many artists "put their hearts out to others" by using the altar as a public instrument of relationship. At the first United Nations Conference on Women held in 1980 in Copenhagen, Betsy Damon built *Shrine for Everywoman.* In the 1980s, too, San Francisco artist Melissa Farley made altars with women who were living with AIDS, and Los Angeles artist Susan Gray created a traveling-altar series called the *Women's History Project.* Gray recorded women's stories of their mothers and grandmothers and left them on

Cristina Biaggi's memorial altar to her mother inspires communication and lasting relationship with this beloved parent.

Over the course of a three-day vigil for peace, Donna Henes accepted gifts from strangers for her *Autumn Altar* (1983) constructed near the Municipal Building in Manhattan.

a portable altar "wall" for others to read or listen to. Currently, Jane Gilmor works with homeless people to create altars that help counter their disenfranchisement.

As a sign of relationship the altar is most effectively used as a place to unite strangers in the common cause of human living. In 1983, during the auspicious days encompassing Halloween, All Saints, and All Souls (31 October to 2 November) Donna Henes, an author and teacher of ritual, created her *Autumn Altar* near the Municipal Building in Manhattan. Made out of cardboard boxes covered with orange fabric, it initially held incense, empty bowls, and fifty-two red glass candles, one for every week of the year. Henes made the altar as a gesture of peace, and she stayed with it continually, day and night, repeating a mantra, "We can all live in peace together, if we want to," and inviting the response of passers-by. People from all walks of life presented things for Donna's altar. Some gave religious items such as miniature Bibles or scapulars. One woman offered the lucky running shorts in which she had never lost a race; another woman gave her eyeglasses; and a teenage boy made and delivered a photomontage of Bob Marley. There were those who simply reached in their pockets to bring a small token of them-selves—pens or cigarettes. Many donated food or money to help others:

The walls of Jane Gilmor's
eight-foot high, house-like
Thank You Shrine (1994–95)
are covered with writings
and drawings of homeless
people from shelters
throughout the USA. The
shrine's hearth altar (detail
shown here) is enclosed by
an inscribed metal border
repeating, "Home is where
the hearth is, home is
where the heart is—home
is where the earth is—
home is where?"

In an effort to unite women from many cultures at the United Nations International Meeting on the Status of Women in Copenhagen, Betsy Damon created *Shrine for Everywoman* (1980).

"People brought sea shells, stones, flowers, fruit, and other food offerings. Lots of people brought food for the needy, foods from their different ethnic traditions. And of course people brought very special stories to tell in front of the altar.... At one point these old Chinese ladies...came by and one of them stopped and looked at the altar and looked at me, then looked at the altar, then looked at me again, and nodded...her approval. She, of course, knew what it was.... All the Asians, Latinos, and Italians...knew what the altar was about; they connected. They joked saying, 'We do that, but ours are more sloppy.' But they loved having a public altar in New York City."

Perhaps what all the participants in Donna's altar understood, either intuitively or through heritage, was a basic sense of the altar's purpose as a place of connection to others. Chole Pescina once said in summarizing her philosophy of altar work: "What I do here goes out to the world. That we may live together, live with care for others and learn to appreciate the life that God gives us. That's the greatest thing He gives us. Life. Living together. And we have to guard it and learn to see that it's the same for everyone." Coming from a different altar practice, Miriam Chamani affirms the same philosophy: "I believe in the universe of the whole…. One essence of expression that expresses through the many *orisha* here on their altars. There is no need for one to dominate. There is a need to understand. The sin that was not cast out was ignorance of the whole, learning to understand each other…. Division is the worst sin. I teach no division, no dissension. Everyone has a feel for the Creator. Everyone. The Creator made everything good."

Chole and Miriam, like so many women who keep the tradition, avow the value of the altar practice as a way to bridge barriers by both symbolizing and enacting the moral righteousness of relationship. Feminist explorations into the psychology of women stress the importance of investigating reconciliation, continuity, affiliation, and relationship as keys to any understanding of women's identity. In the early 1980s, psychologist Carol Gilligan's groundbreaking research on women's moral difference concluded that "women's identity is defined in a context of relationship and judged by a standard of responsibility and care. Similarly, [women's sense of] morality is seen…as arising from the experience of connection and conceived as a problem of inclusion."[1] Gilligan followed Jean Baker Miller, whose earlier studies on women's psychology found that "women's sense of self becomes very much organized around being able to make, and then to maintain, affiliations and relationships…this psychic starting point contains the possibilities for an entirely different (and more advanced) approach to living and functioning… [in which] affiliation is valued as highly as, or more highly than, self-enhancement."[2] Women's profound desire for good relationships, the reliance on connection with others as a source of identity and as a basis for moral judgment and actions, has long been represented and activated in the religious art of personal altars. If, as Gilligan maintains, "women's sense of integrity appears to be entwined with an ethic of care, so that to see themselves as women is to see themselves in a relationship of connection,"[3] the home altar is most certainly a manifestation of this integrity.

CHAPTER FIVE

THE ART OF THE ALTAR

layering, embellishment—and excess

The domestic altar is a woman's artistic as well as her religious expression, and therefore bears evaluation purely in terms of its material arrangement and the motives that this arrangement reveals. The tradition proposes the value of human and divine affiliations as its religious and ethical intention, and this intention is visibly rendered through artistic means. Women's altars promote an *aesthetic of relationship*.

Individual variation in domestic altars is widely apparent, yet there are recognizable features from example to example, even from culture to culture; altars bear a visual and symbolic legacy. As Miriam Chamani explains, the altar's aesthetic is a point of contact between the universal and the personal: "Everyone who understands the universe has her own artistic mind. I am a seeker. The spiritual gives many symbols. The work of the spirit is made exciting through symbols. There is an expression of symbols through each person...." An inventory of typical symbolic objects—both conventional and unconventional—can be drawn up from looking at a number of different women's altars. These objects—some discussed here and the rest in following chapters—both individually and in their arrangement as a group, represent and activate the power of relationship. Gathered around the central divine image, there might be any of the following: multiple prints and statues of secondary religious figures; photos, candles, incense, ritual tools, potions, medicine bundles, shells, crystals, coins, mementos, knick-knacks, gifts, offerings, decorative effects, and even seemingly anomalous items, such as a jar of buttons or a door knob. Some of these things remain fixed for a lifetime, while others may change. The aesthetic of relationship is a dynamic one: expanding, sometimes contracting, then again being replenished over time.

OPPOSITE Layering, accumulation, and embellishment are typical of the home altar's aesthetic properties, seen here in the details of Sra. Cuca Borrego's altar to Niño Fidencio.

The altar's visual aesthetic of relationship is shown in Angela King's photo-image altar dedicated to her mother, her sisters, and her lover—women she says she "must see" with reverence every day.

The condensed—often intense—focus that the altar provides draws its maker into a stimulating visual field. Rabbi Lynn Gottlieb describes the potency of the visible: "the visual focus is important, …it's very hard to create an atmosphere spiritually, internally. The visual aesthetic takes you there right away. Whenever I travel…I make an altar that gives me visual power." Such power lends itself to the immediacy of connection. A glance at her altar invites a woman to catalog the relationships represented there. As Angela King emphasizes, looking is a way of feeling through seeing: "I need to look at my altar. The images that are important, I have to have them out and visible. Accessible. It's all about reverence…to really important beings. And if I don't get to look at them, I can't…survive in this world. I must see them…."

The accessibility of beloved images evokes the reality of beloved relationships. If the first aesthetic goal of an altar is to represent relationship, then the primary artistic move is to set potent images in relation to each other. Rose Wognum Frances explains: "Once you put an object in relation to another, it tells a story; it makes a different reality…. This is the beginning of all art: to take this thing and put it in relation to that thing…always the relationship, the implicit relationship between things. It's the basis of the altar aesthetic…." The sacred space of an altar encloses symbolic objects in a designated frame, a structure that delineates and accentuates the potential for relationship between the human and the Divine. Kathy Vargas explains framing, saying: "To house an image in an altar…establishes a relationship with the sacred, so when you take an object, say a family photograph, and place it in an altar next to a saint, you are basically saying to the saint, 'Pray for this person. Make this family member a part of your holy family.' Putting them in sacred space makes them…accessible to each other." The goal of framing images in sacred space is mediation. Disparate images are shown to intervene on each other's behalf. If the altar is a place for seeking actual intercession with the Divine through prayer and ritual, the altar aesthetic reflects this by visual demonstration. Images enclosed together are poised as intermediaries in, as Kathy Vargas further says, "continuing the conversation" between distinct realities.

The altar advances mediation through the interplay of dimension and intersection: a two-dimensional, horizontal plane (a table, dresser, or other flat surface) holding three-dimensional objects (statues, candles, and so forth) often intersected by a vertical plane, usually a wall, displaying more images. The altar reflects in its structure the potential intercrossing of "heaven" and "earth." Intersection also creates a central point for the image that receives primary veneration. Other items tend to radiate out from that center. Sra. Micaela Zapata's altar was dedicated to the Niño Jesus (the Infant Jesus), and around and behind Him she placed other saints' statues which she referred to as His "celestial court."

The altar's construction induces a kind of ready, vibrating energy, characteristic of the architectural coaction of intersecting and radiating lines. Eclipse has been experimenting with what she calls "altar grids" that are:

The central focus of Sra. Micaela Zapata's altar was the Niño Jesus (Infant Jesus), whose heirloom statue she surrounded with other saints forming what she called His "celestial court."

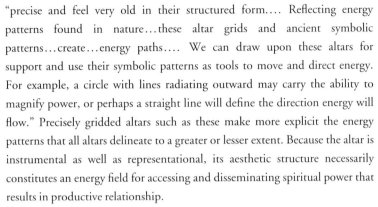

"precise and feel very old in their structured form.... Reflecting energy patterns found in nature...these altar grids and ancient symbolic patterns...create...energy paths.... We can draw upon these altars for support and use their symbolic patterns as tools to move and direct energy. For example, a circle with lines radiating outward may carry the ability to magnify power, or perhaps a straight line will define the direction energy will flow." Precisely gridded altars such as these make more explicit the energy patterns that all altars delineate to a greater or lesser extent. Because the altar is instrumental as well as representational, its aesthetic structure necessarily constitutes an energy field for accessing and disseminating spiritual power that results in productive relationship.

This power flows through the "thingliness" of the altar, its material reality. There objects and symbols are integrated into a coherent visual environment

Elaborate altars dedicated to Niño Fidencio, the Mexican healer and folk saint who lived in the early twentieth century, show the potential of techniques such as layering and accumulation to create an aesthetic of relationship. Over forty years Sra. Florentina Trujillo added objects and images to her beloved saint's altar.

that marks their interdependence and connection with each other. This is achieved through the altar-maker's selection and orchestration of materials, and by her application of certain techniques whereby images and objects that have no immediate affinity are nonetheless yoked together to forge new, interrelated meanings.

In fact, the home altar is the prototype of all women's domestic arts—quilting and appliqué, for example—that evolve from the art-making process that Miriam Schapiro aptly named "femmage."[1] Femmage (a play on "collage" and "assemblage") is women's artistic process of collecting and joining seemingly disparate elements into a functional whole. In making home altars, this method is paramount in realizing the aesthetic of relationship that melds and projects women's chosen social and spiritual values.

Altar-making is process-oriented, and demonstrates what Judith Gleason calls "the priority of piece-work" in women's lives, which allows for "an intermingling of domestic and ceremonial life." She suggests that, "since assemblage is something that happens everywhere in the house, it provides a natural avenue to anthologizing…. Getting it together inwardly and outwardly as one simultaneous process is the therapeutic spin I'd put on endemic women's crafts 'ennobled'…into expositional art." Writer Terry Wolverton further explains that, as women, "Our attention is often scattered over a lot of things, and in short time periods…we pull from a lot of places. This gives us more than one source. We understand how to make use, and make do, with all of what we have. This has to do with being fragmented, and with having to be resourceful, drawing what we need from many sources, not one."

Femmage utilizes the potential of fragmentation as Lucy Lippard defines it: "Fragmentation need not connote explosion, disintegration. It is also a component of networks, stratification, the interweaving of many dissimilar

Sra. Florentina Trujillo brought her daughter Sra. Cuca Borrego (pictured right) into relationship with Niño Fidencio; Cuca established her own home altar to signify her affiliation with the saint.

threads, and de-emphasis on imposed meaning in favor of multiple interpretations.... Fragmentation pervades women's work in all the arts on many subtle levels."[2] Notably heterogeneous, femmage is still rarely unintentional as it drives a cycle that constantly turns fragmentation to wholeness and then back again. As a sacred, symbolic manifestation of this cycle, the home altar demonstrates the value of fragments, which, when linked together, provide a center of focus derived not by imposition, but organically through layering and accretion. This process is described by Candice Goucher: "I think 'accumulation' is a good word to describe the process of acquiring objects that begin to have meaning both in and of themselves and in relation to events or people or places or ideas. The accumulation of objects over time begins to have a power of its own that exceeds the power of the individual object.... Accumulation describes the process of empowerment both for the individual and for the space that [the] altar...occupies." Artist Nancy Fried maintains that layering "is a method for achieving a visual history of the things, the people you care about.... And I do it very carefully. There is a certain kind of history on that altar platform I'm creating—the history of my relationships...." Accumulation and layering promote a kind of benevolent contagion; the significance of one image is lent to another. Lala Treviño is aware of this effect: "You see how I have all different things together here. My Lady of Guadalupe with these little angels. And that doll. It's crazy and they all need dusting. But they all belong together. One thing with the next.... I know each one and how they work together." Images on the altar collectively create an intensification of significance.

Such intensification springs from a process of condensing and miniaturizing. What the scholar and poet Susan Stewart considers as only superficially true of the souvenir collection is authentically true of the home-altar: it "offers transcendence to the viewer" by virtue of "a reduction in physical dimensions corresponding to an increase in significance,...an interiorization of an exterior."[3] As Renee Dooley further notes, the altar employs a microcosmic strategy to gain macrocosmic results: "An altar is a miniature universe, with the mythic elements of creation all present. By learning to see and work with these elements we learn to deal with their expressions in our daily lives."

Condensation and miniaturization are fundamental in making both sacred and social power accessible. A small image of the Virgin of Guadalupe carries her whole history and meaning; a single crystal holds the energy of earth; the feather symbolically recalls the bird's flight; a photograph evokes the presence of a friend. Images on the altar work through substitution and association; the part stands for the whole, like attracts like. The aesthetic of relationship is dependent upon the way selected objects reveal "dimensions of similarity" in both metonymic and metaphoric ways. Storyteller Jay Goldspinner interprets this as the way in which the altar aesthetic affirms "the relation between the physical and the spiritual world, the minute and the infinite, the microcosm-macrocosm."

Whether discovered in a loosely defined or a highly ordered scheme, miniaturization, fragment-ation, accretion, and layering are aesthetic modes that create an overall quality both receptive and embracing. The aesthetic of relationship idealizes growth, abundance, and inclusion. Nancy Fried says, "Part of layering…is this idea that you always get more; you can always have more. Altars are about more. Altars are packed. Accumulation is about having flexibility to make something work. If you don't get it here—you get it here." The additive process results in a tendency toward excess, a creative layering of objects that simultaneously evokes many relationships, many meanings—religious, familial, personal, political. Things ride up against each other and are positioned in relation to each other, creating a stacked, overlapping, montage effect. Chole Pescina taped a photograph of President Kennedy

Above her altar, Chole Pescina collaged images of the Virgin, President Kennedy, and a photo of her cousins to show that "they belong together." The home altar's aesthetic of relationship symbolically unites distinct domains of concern in a woman's life.

John Fitzgerald Kennedy

and a snapshot of her two cousins on to a picture of the Virgin hanging above her altar table. Chole asserted, "I put them all together to show that they belong together. The Virgin takes care of everyone. She doesn't say 'yes' to one and 'no' to another." As Chole suggests, the altar aesthetic composes an ever-inclusive family of images. The meeting of signs and symbols representing the different domains of a woman's life is a visible statement of her claim that they are ideally interrelated. With divine help, her devotion brings this claim to fruition in the world beyond her altar.

The loading of the altar space also allows for the repetition of certain beloved images. On Bereniece Alvarado's altar there are a number of versions of Our Lady of Guadalupe, each slightly different; Jayanthi Raman's altar to Durga displays many copies of the Goddess's image lined up in rows. Multiple images often represent gifts from those who know the altar-maker's

A Catholic all her life, Margarita Guerrero still found it easy to incorporate an image of the Buddha on her altar.

Indigo Mercy (1975) by Betye Saar reflects her understanding of the altar as a place for integrating diverse images and materials.

heightened relationship with a particular deity. Certainly reiteration points to favoritism. As Sra. Alvarado says, "All the Virgins are the same, but…Guadalupe is more familiar, more beautiful…. I tell my daughter to buy Her for my birthday and she does…." Sra. Alvarado's many Guadalupes are signs of her familiarity and intimacy with this aspect of the Virgin. They are testimonies to a grateful and dedicated devotion, imparting a dramatic visual sense of the effectiveness of relationship with a beloved deity.

Through these modes of layering, accumulation, condensation, and repetition, the aesthetic of relationship pushes towards integration. The altar is a place where union overrides distinction just as relationship overcomes separation. For example, sacred images may represent participation in one particular religious culture—Mexican Catholicism or Goddess Spirituality—but in many cases women's altars reflect an absorption of several religious traditions through an array of objects that reveal a love of diversity. This diversity is then reinvested in a strategy of creative integration; the appeal is to the whole, to the way the altar joins like with like, but also like with unlike. On her Mexican-Catholic altar, Margarita Guerrero kept an image of the Buddha given to her by a friend's daughter. His presence was completely acceptable, not in doctrinal but in relational terms: "I don't know his prayers, but he keeps company with the Virgin." In artist Dominique Mazeaud's altar room, among the many images from different traditions, there is a painting of Kali and Our Lady of Guadalupe drinking coffee together at the kitchen table. Betye Saar, in altar-making as in life, recognizes the importance of "Integration. First, the creative energy with the materials, and then the work of integrating the materials themselves—diverse materials which are old or new, from one or another culture.... I try to resolve the problem of integration in my art. This is the task of most women in our lives...[but] I am also talking about black and white integration. I had acknowledged and unacknowledged white relatives, an interracial marriage, children who are both black and white. All this is part of my self-structure. Integration means a global perspective...." Altar objects assist a woman's own sense of integration as it evolves in a dialectic between the personal and the universal, between autobiography and history, between people and cultures, as well as between heaven and earth. This dialectic is fueled by the altar's aesthetic of relationship, which visually expresses a unification of distinct forces and realities represented in a harmonious blending of their symbols.

The aesthetic of relationship is further served by embellishment. Twinkling lights, plastic and hand-made flowers, streamers, doilies, veils, and ribbons create a visual profusion that accords with the central goal of personal devotion, both explicit and implicit, of increase and generation. Some women take embellishment to dramatic extremes. In her public altar installations, artist Patssi Valdez often purposely overstates the alluring properties of embellishment. In one example, Valdez engulfed a small image of the Virgin with rococo bursts of florid decoration. As Bereniece Alvarado makes quite clear, "You have to decorate. Well, I do, anyway. I keep adding things to make it more beautiful. To show how good life is. It's like my garden. I keep putting in plants because I like to see things grow."

A pleasing visual environment helps make the altar a desirable place, both for its creator and for her deities. Decorative materials enhance the altar's possibilities for communication. Their texture, glitter, and bright colors— their visual vitality—provide an inducement for focusing on the power made available at the altar. In fact, embellishments are often used to draw attention to favored images as well as to index their prestige. Encrusted with decoration, they are adored through beautification because they have "proven" the effectiveness of relationship with them over time. Suzi Gablik's Black Madonna "is festooned with charms and amulets.... From her neck trail rosaries of red and blue glass beads, antique Christmas beads and ornaments, clusters of bells, feathers, a good luck charm...from Japan, a

Celtic female deity…and various other amulets received as gifts. At her feet is a heap of dried flowers, beads, pods, talismans, crystals, …small goddess figurines, and a tiny pair of red, sequined dancing shoes, like Dorothy's in *The Wizard of Oz*." Embellished icons are distinguished from all others. They are invested with the riches of amulets, ornaments, and other gifts to proclaim the richness of relationship with the deities that they represent.

Seasonal decorations, often ephemeral in nature, are added on religious holidays or to mark significant events in the altar-maker's life, which, of course, include important occasions for the members of her family. A statue of Our Lady of Guadalupe is surrounded by cut-felt poinsettias on her feast day in early December. An altar to the Great Goddess is heaped with corn at harvest time. Sra. Romualda Perez's daughters load her altar with the souvenirs and baubles of their teenage activities (corsages, cards, balloons, and pom-poms). She occasionally sweeps it clean, but only as she says, "to make room for more." The appearance and disappearance of ephemeral decorations mark time and occasion, but just as often they accumulate to become fixed aspects of the overloaded visual display.

In so many ways, the altar sustains its visual and material purpose as an expression of surplus. However, its bounty would be meaningless and its intentions would be void were it not for the gifts and collaborations at the heart of the altar-making aesthetic. Women's altars are replete with gifts that actively signify the value of relationships, and each gift—whether given by family or friends to the altar-maker, or by the altar-maker to her deities—records a material understanding of that value.

Gifts help establish the altar's emotional atmosphere of trust, intimacy, remembrance, and alliance. Sarah Johnson's altar holds, among other things, an arrowhead given to her by her husband, a silk scarf from her cousin, an African Goddess figure brought to her by her brother, and a bowl from her sister: "These things center me…and remind me of the support I have from friends and…siblings…. Each item stirs in me a connection to others…." Shelley Anderson remarks on the way gifts placed on the altar acknowledge—even help overcome—cultural or religious difference:

Patssi Valdez emphasizes the alluring properties of embellishment in *Altar Installation at Plaza de La Raza* (1993) by overstating the altar's visual attractiveness in a rococo burst of florid decoration applied around a small image of the Virgin.

"On the wall of the alcove where our altar is located, I nailed a small handwoven bag. Inside the bag is a small block, pressed from earth gathered at Mecca. A friend, returning from Iran, gave it to me as a gift. Aware of the many misunderstandings Westerners have of Islam, she asked only that I treat it with respect. To honor her wish I placed it above our altar."

Norma Joyce's altar to the Goddess holds an image of Wonder Woman given to her by her daughter.

In traditional contexts especially, sacred images are circulated through inheritance, as signs of irreversible bonding between mothers and daughters. Like many others, Chelo Gonzalez and Margarita Guerrero were each given saints' images by their mothers. In a less typical but telling example, Women's Spirituality advocate Norma Joyce received an unusual image for her altar from her daughter: "My daughter, Jane-Ellen, gave me Wonder Woman and it was a very special gift. She was about thirteen when I gave her a copy of the Wonder Woman book, and I inscribed it 'to a wonder woman.' …And when she found this plastic Wonder Woman, she gave it to me. An important exchange between Mother and Daughter."

Gifts in the form of offerings are used to honor or entreat relationship with divine beings or to show thanks for blessings received from them. Chelo Gonzalez regularly puts fresh roses before the Virgin: "These flowers are my gift to Her—the ones she likes best." Similarly, Calelmmirre Quelle makes her routine offerings to the Goddess and God of her Pagan beliefs: "Whenever I find something during the day that is natural, a walnut, a feather, a pretty stone, a little extra bread, or berry, I place it in the offering basket…to thank the Goddess and God for their gift to me." As a repository of gifts given to deities for blessings received from them, the altar is a model of the exchange critical to the productivity of any relationship, human or divine.

The effectiveness of this model is emphasized in specialized home altars made primarily for the purpose of recognizing divine relationships through gifting with food. Charged with associations of earth, fertility, nurturance,

Friends of Sally Cantarella help arrange and dress her St Joseph's Day altar.

heat, and home, food is an unequaled offering of the feminine to the Divine made, for example, in the Mexican-American tradition for the Day of the Dead, in the Sicilian-American tradition for St. Joseph's Day, in Wicca for certain sabbats, in African *orisha* traditions for the ancestors, and in Hindu tradition for feast days for Goddess Durga or Goddess Lakshmi. The mounds of home-made cakes, candies, and cookies layered on St. Joseph's altars are presented in ritual thanks for spiritual sustenance received from the saints, but these offerings also propel a cycle of human exchange: women donate their labor of food-preparation to the altar-giver; she in turn uses the food they have made to fête Sicilian community members who attend the celebration at her home. Finally, at the close of the feast day, any leftover food is given to needy strangers (for example, the indigent elderly in a nursing-home), completing the cycle. In a symbolic sense, women feed the whole world from their St. Joseph's altars. They dramatically exemplify a universal axiom of women's devotion. Within both the human and sacred worlds, women nourish productive and lasting relationships within a daily process of exchange, of giving and receiving. As the circulation of festival foods makes clear, the women's altar tradition is not about simply displaying or holding the symbols of power, but about distributing them; at the altar, giving and receiving are commensurate.

This leads to consideration of what might be called the "economics" of the altar. Its aesthetic of relationship urges acceptance of a religiously grounded paradox: this site of material accumulation serves the circulation of spiritual riches. Looking at her altar, Micaela Zapata proudly proclaimed, "This is my source of wealth." She of course referred to the richness of her faith represented there. The altar's aesthetic promotes a show of spiritual wealth, yet generally it does so with materials that are negligible in terms of actual cost. Humble and "lesser" material objects are assigned a context where they represent a surplus of significance. Even the most seemingly anomalous or expendable things—a garden trowel, a hospital identification bracelet, a child's stuffed animal, a stone, a postcard—can be invested with a deeper obligation than might be apparent. Such unusual "icons," in fact, fit the aesthetic of the personal altar quite well; the power of relationship embraces items that formally do not suit the scheme. The creative should override the con-ventional, as Judith Gleason discovered through her friendship with Sunta, a Santería practitioner in the Bronx: "Sunta's example taught me that upon even the tacky can be predicated spiritual meaning. Anything that glitters can be gold. A plastic whirligig be wind. Through pipes in the bathroom flows the river of the dead; cotton wicks placed in a bowl upon the linoleum floor may portend the volcano." Obviously, the altar's economy of spiritual "riches" does not refer to market value, but to great symbolic value, freely accruing in an environment of full and dynamic creative independence. The aesthetic of relationship cannot be *bought* in objects, it can only be *stored* in their accu-mulation and arrangement. As gauges of belief, memory, emotion, experience, and transformation, objects lastingly refer to the immeasurable worth of actual relationships and their effect on the altar-maker. Perhaps this is why altar displays tend toward excess; an abundance of desire and need for others is matched by an overflow of items that indicate both the reality of, and the hope for, the benefits of continuing affiliations.

Finally, the aesthetic of the altar embeds a woman's own understanding of the potency of beauty. Artist Nancy Fried states, "I make altars out of total necessity. I make them because they symbolize spirituality...and transformation. But it's also about beauty.... And the beauty of altars is the most important thing in the world. Without beauty, we are dead. An altar acknowledges the power of beauty." Margot Adler views the altar as an "encounter" with beauty. This condensed microcosm of beautiful things reflects and makes available the all-pervasive beauty of the macrocosm—nature, divine reality, the universe: "A lot of what women bring to an altar is beautiful.... It's an encounter with beauty. When I look at what I have here on my altar—the shells, images...it's all beautiful...these things, each one of them can take me to a story, to a contemplation of beauty, of the beauty of nature, of the beauty which is...part of divine reality. So we have a place for the contemplation of the spiritual, but also the contemplation of the beauty of the universe.... It's a coming to an encounter with beauty, a coming to an encounter with creativity...." Beauty revealed at the altar is not removed from everyday life as a limited category of objective aesthetic worth; rather, it is encountered subjectively in moments of simple recognition, as Yemaya Wind explains: "There is something about walking into a room and then, there it is.... It's a kind of beauty that you set up. You designate the power of that beauty." Beauty is made available by a woman's own recognition of its presence, a presence she has consciously invited and created. The preciousness of certain objects—beloved images, gifts—associates beauty with intimacy.

Margarita Guerrero's love for the Virgin of San Juan is based in belief, but also in visual pleasure: "All the saints have their reason for being. But the Virgin is the one who has the most beauty. She shines like a star. She is brilliant. She fascinates." Her physical beauty makes the Virgin all the more available, more attracting, more real. The Virgin's beauty is a sign of Her unlimited power of presence in Sra. Guerrero's life. A sense of beauty diminishes distance between a woman and the Divine. At the altar, beauty is a startling realization of the interpenetration of the material with the spiritual. And this realization can happen over and over again at this place where beauty is never used up but is constantly enlivened in aesthetic processes that are lent to relationship, remembrance, and renewal.

The beauty of women's altars signals a sense of the aesthetic project that centers on an impulse toward wholeness. The altar aesthetic is based on connection and interdependence. It artfully renders the specifics of women's experiences, perceptions, and values, and thereby makes a claim for their specific validity, even as, and because, they differ from dominant values and perceptions.

In her book, *The Reenchantment of Art* (1992), Suzi Gablik argues for a new view of art and a new model of aesthetics. Suggesting that currently the artist is privileged as an "egocentric, 'separative' self, whose perfection lies in absolute independence from the world," she calls for a yielding to the "feminine value of relatedness." She asserts: "Art has been organized around the primacy of objects rather than relationships, and has been set apart from reciprocal or participative interactions.... To reverse this priority, giving primacy to relationships and interaction, is also to reverse the way that artists see their role, and implies a radical deconstruction of the aesthetic mode itself...freedom might lie less in the solipsistic ideal of doing whatever one wants, and more in the accomplishment of 'bringing into relationship.' "[4] Gablik's call has already been answered in the art of the women's altar where the power of beauty releases the power of relationship.

CHAPTER SIX

Annapurna's Hindu-style
altar is a place to seek
God by seeing God
embodied in images
of divine teachers such
as Ramakrishna.

THE POWER OF IMAGES
embodiment and identification

The previous chapter focused on the aesthetics of the altar as they concern its purely material aspects, but the aesthetic of relationship that the home altar proposes in its physical arrangement points to something else: the lived relationship with those holy personages symbolically housed at the altar site. The altar is a context for evoking active affiliation with sacred beings, and all its conventional and invented aesthetic and artistic qualities are lent to this purpose.

The aesthetic of relationship nourishes an intimacy, a sense of receptivity, that grounds a woman's most crucial attachment to a primary deity, who is generally represented at the altar's center in the form of a particularly beloved statue, picture, or photo. For Gloria Rocha, the central icon is the Virgin of San Juan; for Heather Fox, it is Aphrodite; and for Suzi Gablik, the Black Madonna. For these women, and others, sacred representations are not merely material objects; they evoke embodied subjects. Since the beginning of religious consciousness, the goddesses and gods have been evoked in bodily human-like form. Evocation—the summoning of a deity or spirit—is the first function of religious icons.

Sacred icons are unique in their ability to mediate the difference between the human and the Divine by proposing a similarity between the human body and the divine body. This has resulted in a dilemma, the problem of idolatry, which has confounded religious philosophy for centuries. Can a material image be said to come alive with the potency of divine power? That women have answered this question affirmatively is at the heart of the home-altar tradition.

Home altars are abundantly populated with sacred body images indicating women's essential desire to bring the spiritual and physical together through the body as the chief source of knowing and being known. Relationship explicitly claims the primacy of embodiment; relationship is founded in the body and between bodies. According to the historian Mircea Eliade, religious images are kinds of *hierophanies*, or modes of the sacred. Other *hierophanies* include myths and rites, but what is important to realize is that the sacred is "always manifested through something…the sacred expresses itself through something other than itself; it appears in things, myths, or symbols, but never wholly or directly."[1] In bodily images the sacred is conveyed with visible, palpable directness; it is literally and figuratively "fleshed out." Most important, the sacred is *socialized* through the body and brought into the world of human interaction where it can have an effect on the daily course of living.

With a most profound sense of intimacy and affection, women socialize the sacred body at their altars. Altar-makers clearly understand and are attracted to the bodily potency of divine images. Their human—and hence their sensory—portrayal, with mouths, ears, eyes, and open arms implies their readiness to communicate, to both listen and respond. In turn, images are treated as bodies by being invited into relationship through speech, gesture, touch, emotion, and feeling—through an engagement with the "person" in the "body" of the image.

Embodiment encourages personification. Personifying avails what Jungian psychologist James Hillman has called an "epistemology of the heart." "Personifying…offers another venue of loving, of imagining things in personal form so that we can find access to them with our hearts.… Personifying emotionalizes.… Loving is a way of knowing, and for loving to know, it must personify."[2] For altar-makers, personifying the sacred is a practiced religious mode of belief and loving, which recognizes the bodily image of divine beings as a locus of intimacy and trust—the body as a vessel for intimate communication. Personifying overcomes difference; it becomes the activity of incorporating Otherness through a process of deeply felt identification and alliance. Body and spirit achieve an integration that makes each available to, and co-dependent with, the other.

But personifications at the altar are never simply projections. By personifying the sacred bodily image a woman transforms it—transubstantiates it—into a living presence. What a woman thus accomplishes at the altar site is no less than an act of creation. Vicki Noble suggests that women are particularly adept at giving form to spirit. While pregnant with her son, she made a feathered image of Lilith, protector of women in childbirth: "I felt it was kind of a call to bring her into form...when you bring something into form like this then the spirit can come into it, whatever the entity is...it can come into this physical form and live there....Women...access the divine through the visionary mind; once you have it in form, then it starts talking to you."

In her Hindu practice, Annapurna has learned what she calls "intuitive seeing at the altar." This is, as she says, based on the need to "see god, not just seek god." She explains: "We have taken the subject and objectified it for the purpose of becoming one with the subject...the idea is that when you come to the altar in the Hindu faith, one of the first things you do is acknowledge that pure consciousness cannot be looked at—we automatically objectify it [in image form] because we have a different mind, but we acknowledge that.... In the case of really blessed worshipers like Ramakrishna, the image literally comes alive because of their total devotion—it becomes a living image that others can feel. And that is really the purpose of worship, that through your loving attention, the image comes alive and that may not appear to the outer eye; it may only appear in your heart and it may come and go depending upon the intensity of your devotion and the purity of your mind."

Sheri Tornatore, whose altar features the Virgin Mary, explains how her sense of a spiritual relationship with the Virgin is mediated through Her bodily icon: "Most of us look at a statue or a picture and we know it's just that, but we don't want it to be just that. It's our link. Even though it's made out of stone, it's not just stone—it's spirit.... With Mary, I hope that she will some day envelop me physically, and take me in her robes. That I will feel this incredible sense of transcendence—both physical and spiritual—they are the same. It is physical. It's a hope for physicality.... The altar is a place to practice that hope.... It's like when you think of someone all the time and you realize you want to be with that person. Their physical presence is important.... A relationship with Mary is a relationship. It's real.... The statue is representational, but the relationship to Her is real through that. And that's what altars are for...when you put the Rosary to your lips you are caressing Her. If you believe strongly enough, you really are kissing Her. It's not a thing anymore, it becomes a presence. In the moment." Particularly at her own altar, a woman feels the presence—the sensual personhood—of the Divine. Spirit is assumed to be in the body, not absent from it, and sensation becomes a source of intelligence, meaning, and belief.

Sheri Tornatore spent over a year creating her wall-size *Devotional Altar for Mary* (1994), which embodies her love for the Virgin and recalls her grandmother's similar devotion: "I wanted to know what the presence of Mary meant for me and my grandmother and other people I loved.... Because I believe that She really does exist, that She comes down and talks to people."

OPPOSITE BELOW At the very center of Chole Pescina's altar is the worn, chipped, 100-year-old statue of San Antonio that has been her source of relationship with the saint she familiarly calls "Tonio."

The occurrence through which a sacred image comes to have a bodily presence for a woman can happen very early, even in childhood. Gloria Rocha, speaking of her attraction to the image of the Virgin of San Juan, pointed to a faded picture of the Virgin which she has had since she was nine years old: "You see, I had this one when I was a little girl.... Somebody in Mexico give it to my mother.... I take it and put it in my room. And from then She's been close. All the time She's been close." The moment of an impending embodied relationship with the Divine may occur in a flash of visceral epiphany as it did for Suzi Gablik: "I had no particular religious beliefs, nor was I on any spiritual path, when I found my Black Madonna in a store in Santa Barbara...as I saw her from the doorway, my body registered the electric shock of something pregnant with fate.... Little did I realize...that my relationship with this divine figure would...become a conduit for the unfolding of a powerful mythic journey in my life.... Significant mythic journey often begins at a point when the very act of seeking sets something in motion to meet us...something in the universe responds, as if to an invitation." "Something in the universe responds" through an incarnation—through a bodily representation. It provokes in the seeker a bodily response—the "shock" of recognition that a relationship has begun.

ABOVE Suzi Gablik's altar to the Black Madonna is charged with the living presence of divine female energy.

Other women testify that their close relationship with certain images was conveyed to them by their mothers or grandmothers. Most important of the saints on Chole Pescina's altar was a very old statue of San Antonio, which had

belonged to her grandmother. Chole's intimate relationship with this saint was revealed in her familiar approbation of him as "Tonio" or "Tonito": "We learned to believe in all the saints. Principally Jesus, Mary and Joseph. Foremost—right? But Tonio was the one who held on to Christ and said, 'I won't let go.' He grants us everything. Everything good." When she was a young girl, Sra. Margarita Guerrero was given a statue of the Virgin of San Juan by her grandmother, who told her to care for it, to dress it, to celebrate and adore it. In essence, she was taught to "mother" the bodily representation of the Virgin. Sra. Guerrero kept this image all her life, and when she became a midwife in her later years, the statue "assisted" her in many births: "Love for the Virgin is a mother's love. A mother understands. And I will tell you how. When I was a midwife I always brought my statue of the Virgin of San Juan with me to the woman. Now if you look at this statue, it's nothing. It's even dirty and old. But to me it's beautiful. It is the Mother. And so I bring it so the mother could be with this Mother. And I would have her kiss the Virgin to help her. And they would be together. Because this little statue is a mother, too. The best Mother. She understands the pain, but She also gives the happiness."

Embodied in a worn old statue, the Divine Mother is made the living partner of a human mother in bringing other bodies to life. If, as artist Carolyn Oberst suggests, "Women understand…image veneration in a visceral way," this is true in great part because the physical labors and entailments of pregnancy, birth, breast-feeding, and child-rearing can be shared with a Divine Mother whose visible, familiar body in image form is a source of desirable identification. In this way, reproductive processes are assisted; moreover, by extension, a woman's body—her life lived in the body—is validated; her capacity to regenerate human life is made sacred.

A woman's sense of suffering, whether her own or the suffering of others, also can impel active affiliation with the embodied Divine. After all, it is the loneliness of suffering, felt in such a real way through the body, either physically or emotionally, which creates the need for relationship to other bodies, including divine bodies. Shortly after her wedding, Casey Covarrubias's mother gave her a statue of Guadalupe so that she could start an altar in her new home. But Casey wanted a "modern life" and she put the statue away in a closet. Years had passed when Casey entered a period of her life that was filled with misgivings: "I was so depressed and one day I got out that statue that Mama gave to me and…I started carrying that statue everywhere with me and talking to Our Lady. I used to take it out to walk around the block and I used to put it by my bed to sleep at night. And, you know, I started to feel better. And I told my husband I wanted to make an altar for Her…. It's my—what would you call it—my therapy. *Anglos* go to the therapist and we go to Our Lady of Guadalupe." The statue of Our Lady had been little more to her than the static representation of her Catholic upbringing, but on those walks around the block, Casey embraced embodied affiliation with the Virgin. She came to the Virgin with her body and the body of the Virgin, in the form of this statue, gave back Casey's life in her body.

Co-dependency between a woman and her special images is fostered in time spent together on a daily basis, either in religious activity such as prayer, or even in the most mundane moments. Mrs. Angelike Manolakis found companionship with a small image of Christ, which she often removed from her *eikonostasio* so He might accompany her on her daily rounds: "He is my favorite—my darling. I take Him shopping with me, I talk to Him, because none of the others look at me like Him—see? He looks! Every morning after I cense the *eikonostasio*, I take Him with me, put Him on the kitchen table and I have my coffee with him. I say, 'Good morning, how are you?' " As Mrs. Manolakis confirms, a particular image is singled out not only by the woman's intention, but also by the intention of the image itself. The icon of Christ "looks" at Mrs. Manolakis like no other; His gaze confirms their mutual affection. Between people, eye contact establishes the desire to interact, and between icon and believer there is an equal need to signal the attention and attentiveness of one to the other. The history of religious icons is full of legendary testimony concerning their ability to move, speak, look, bleed, and weep. Their embodiment is not only figurative; it is believed to be literal. Belief is in fact confirmed in divine demonstrations of bodily vitality.

Such vitality is described in loving, concrete detail. In fact, it is made all the more real through the concrete. Embodiment reifies physical particulars;

personification evokes personality. Relationship with divine beings is based not in abstraction or generality, but in the daily details of shared experience that result in trust and commitment. Aina Olomo's love for Shangó is passionately affirmed in her lived appreciation of all of his physical and emotional attributes. She *knows* him: "He's the thunder god. He fights for social causes; he's a warrior. He's an administrator.... He's charismatic. He likes people.... He's that spark that is intellect. He's passion—the imagery of fire. That's his momentum in the world. The world would be an awful place without his energy. First of all it would be dark. There wouldn't be any light. Couldn't eat 'cause you couldn't cook. Wouldn't have any sex 'cause he's also a very sexual *orisha*. Life would be quite boring without his energy.... And Shangó tends to be a little obstinate, a little rebellious. He does what he wants to do.... The question has been asked of me...do you still want to continue this journey? And my answer—Absolutely!...He's a great mate. A great mate.... He has always made me be more than I ever thought was possible.... The longer I live with Shangó, the more he amazes me.... This is my relationship.... The one I've got. And I love him." Aina's relationship with Shangó is articulated through the symbolic language of marriage, which affirms its physicality. The union of their bodies makes their spiritual journey together possible—and all the more "amazing."

Kathleen Alexander-Berghorn's Hindu altar embodies the Goddess Saraswati and her living incarnation, Mataji, the altar-maker's guru.

In a very different tradition, Hinduism, incarnation of this kind also allows for a relationship to deity that is progressively intensified through deepening awareness of the interpenetration of body and spirit. At her altar, Kathleen Alexander-Berghorn daily invites the presence of Goddess Saraswati and her living manifestation, Guru Mataji. Both are considered incarnate in their images, a statue of the goddess and a photo of the guru: "Saraswati, goddess of inspiration, wisdom, and the creative arts, is the aspect of the Divine Mother I have chosen as my spiritual ideal or *Ishta*. My altar is dedicated to my *Ishta*, or 'Beloved,' and to my spiritual teacher, whom I look upon as Her embodiment. The identification of the *Ishta* with the Teacher and the realization of their essential oneness with each other and with the worshiper herself is a tenet of Indian religious thought which is especially meaningful to me as a woman and a devotee of the Divine Mother. I feel…privileged that my Guru is a woman…whom I call Mataji, meaning 'Mother.' Although the illumined soul transcends all sexual boundaries, it is very inspiring for me to have an opportunity to see the inherent divinity of women manifest in a woman who has attained conscious identity with the Divine Mother…. My altar, in a corner of my bedroom, is for me the home of the Divine Mother…. In contemplating…images of the Goddess I am worshiping the Reality behind the form; yet for me the image itself is a manifestation of Spirit…. All the symbolic attributes conveyed by the images of Saraswati are embodied for me in my Teacher, whose picture is the focal point of my altar. Through her life and being Mataji manifests for me the attributes of my *Ishta*…. Mataji embodies the love and compassion of the Divine Mother…." In Kathleen's veneration of Guru Mataji, her photograph is alive with the visceral reality of her teacher and Saraswati.

Photographic portraits such as Kathleen's of Mataji allow for a particularly potent evocation of divine embodiment. The invention of photography radically altered the human ability to produce, process, and absorb images of all kinds. Specifically with regard to religion, it made possible the documentation and image-replication of "living saints," such as the Hindu Ramakrishna, the Tibetan Buddhist Dalai Lama, and, in the Catholic tradition, Bernadette of Lourdes, Mother Cabrini, and El Niño Fidencio, a renowned Mexican healer who lived in the early part of this century. Photographs of these spiritual intermediaries exhibit a continuity with universal religious images, the age-old paintings and sculptures of the Virgin, of the Buddha, of Kali, or of the Goddess. However, photographed bodies render an even more explicit relational quality; they are closer to the actual, the particular bodies of the holy beings they represent. Photographic icons uniquely mediate the gap between the human and the Divine—in fact, the Divine is made all the more intimate, more real by virtue of such documentation.

When, at her altar, a woman endows an image of the Divine with person-hood, she chooses an intimate relationship for her own needs and purposes. The body-based nature of relationship as it is established at the altar site is crucial to women's sense of identity. Artifacts on the altar are embodiments of the maker, not just representations of a religious system. Practitioners of Goddess Spirituality have made this especially clear. Their veneration of female images poses a direct challenge to the patriarchally ordained symbolic order. These women love the body of the Goddess whose enforced absence and devaluation under patriarchy is radically reformulated by them. Reclaiming the Goddess has, more than anything else, been a reclaiming of the female body as a site of sacred power and positive identification. For Heather Fox, affiliation with Aphrodite reverses the classic deformation of this deity as an objectified "sex goddess" to a subjectively understood creative and

Heather Fox, whose altar is dedicated to Aphrodite, follows a Goddess-centered, woman-identified spirituality which upholds the sacredness of the female body.

healing personification: "Aphrodite, the central image of my personal altar, represents the healing power of the feminine principle…. Working with Her seems to stimulate my creativity and deep dreaming, to strengthen bonds with other women, to enhance my ability to love my body and appreciate its beauty, to know my body as the temple of the Goddess…. I've come to realize that She is far more than the harlot or whore that patriarchy would make of her…. But most of all, I am in touch with the depth of Her healing to my spirit and the ways in which this healing manifests on a physical level. Her image has been very empowering to my healing process."

In my observation, most home altars have at their center a feminine aspect of the Divine. Whether directed to an image of the Virgin Mary or Goddess Aphrodite, devotion to sacred feminine embodiments confirms the value that women place on their own embodiment, their own bodies. Offering a profound critique of the manner in which Western philosophy and theology associate women's bodies with sin, impurity, and the "lesser" material and natural realms, women's esteem for and devotion to the incarnate status of female deities subverts this devaluation in favor of a different conception of the female body. At her altar a woman engages the female body—hers and the deity's—as an agent of creativity, relationship, intelligence, and feeling—of autonomy as well.

Religious icons are open to wider interpretations than religious texts, and, historically, women have used this fact to their advantage. Medievalist Caroline Walker Bynum contends that the different use of religious symbols by women and men is promoted through their ability to "speak" differently to different audiences. Meaning is then "not so much imparted as appropriated in a dialectical process whereby it becomes subjective reality for the one who uses the symbol."[3] When women make their relationships to divine images private and domestic, these images undergo a creative manipulation. An altar-maker's deliberate appropriation stimulates her special relationship with the image of her choosing; its subjective and embodied status is something she alone assigns and interprets.

The embodied love of an image is based foremost on identification—one body finding in the image of another a source of truly being known. This is nowhere more apparent than in instances where a secular image is given central importance on an altar. For Daphne LeSage the "image" of singer Barbra Streisand embodies the qualities of self-determination that Daphne sought in herself: "My Barbra Streisand altar is for this very powerful person in my life. When I was married, I played "Funny Girl" over and over again. I sang it. Barbra connected me to who I really was. Who I became." Here the "religious" value—the transformative power—of an image is not linked to religion *per se*, but solely to the altar-maker's desire for self-identity. In creating altars to popular figures—Madonna, Frida Kahlo, Princess Diana—women sacralize the secular for their own purposes of self-knowledge and self-understanding. Meanings are subjective, invented, imagined—not imposed.

In our era women are constantly expanding the range and flexibility of religious images. For Shamaan Ochaum, whose primary image is Mother Earth, the "body" centrally represented on her altar is a portion of the Earth's body: "I would have something born of the Earth Mother, in the form created by the Earth Mother. A left-handed crystal for example.... The left-handed crystal is attuned to the feminine, the intuitive. I would have a wonderful, smoky, left-handed crystal as a representative of that earth energy. To me, that is a step closer to the source than a figure.... My sense of the image is not figural but elemental: of fire, water, earth, of air...when I'm going through my day here in the city, it is critical to have something that says, 'I know She's come,' as a result of my saying, 'Help.' Being responded to with a sign of Earth on my altar that says, 'I'm Here.' "

Altars dedicated to secular "saints" are exemplified by Daphne LeSage's altar to Barbra Streisand.

Nancy Blair felt called to redeem ancient images of the Goddess when she was studying male-biased art history in graduate school: "When I first saw a reproduction of the Willendorf Goddess, I got goose-bumps. My imagination was stirred by Her 'presence.' I felt an inexplicable, yet profound sense of 'belonging.' ...Some 'ancient memory' had been sparked and I knew one thing: I had to have Goddess images around me and with me all the time. I wanted to remind myself every day...that at one time, long ago, having been born female was a sacred blessing and honor. I feverishly began 'reproducing' Goddesses, modeling them carefully and precisely, making them as close to the original artifact as possible. I felt like a priestess, an emissary of the Goddess. I felt like Lilith, who returned to Her Motherland by the Red Sea, producing a hundred children just like Her every day! I thought if I could just recreate *all* the ancient Goddesses, no one could take them away from me ever again." Blair's images of the Goddess are purchased by women all over the world: "I offer these images as a healer offers her

herbs, chants and visions to the community for both personal and collective healing. Ultimately, I make Goddess images as my contribution to transformational 'wholing' of lopsided ideologies and theologies where women and women's spiritual values are marginalized, denied, and ignored. Mine is an art of teaching, healing, and linking; making accessible what was once covered and denied. The Goddess images I create affirm and validate our power as women by joining our spiritual heritage, myths, and mystery with possibilities of personal identification and immanent potentialities for the present and future. I make each Goddess as a reminder, a mnemonic art of what was, what is and what can be. An act of alchemical transformation; turning something into something else, Earth into Fire, matter into spirit.... My creativity is not

Shamaan Ochaum assumes the possibility of embodied relationship with Mother Earth in the form of a smoky crystal at the center of her private altar.

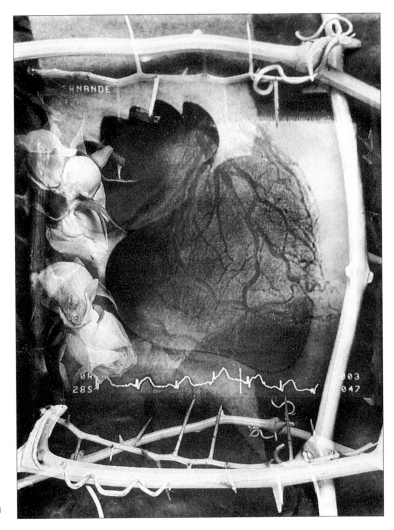

Kathy Vargas's early attraction to the Sacred Heart, stimulated by traditional statues of the image brought from Mexico in the early 20th century by her grandmother, eventually inspired her series of hand-colored, multi-layered photographic altars revealing the heart alone. *Cuerpo de Milagros* (Body of Miracles, 1995) was made for a friend who suffered a heart attack; his EKG reading is integrated into the altar.

about *me*: I am a conduit. I tell my friends: 'I was bitten by Her bee.' I work for the Queen."

Kathy Vargas and another Texas artist, Connie Arismendi, have both reworked traditional images of the Mexican version of the Sacred Heart of Jesus. Devotion to the Sacred Heart has a long tradition in Vargas's family.

She grew up with statues of the Sacred Heart brought by her grandmother from Mexico when her family emigrated from there years ago: "I fell in love with the Sacred Heart as a young adolescent. If I had problems I always went to Him. It's because of that heart image. His robe is open.... The image is about feeling and emotion, our yearnings for love...because he's got this exposed heart. What could be a more volatile image in a sense, than an exposed heart?" In her photo-

In this votive painting called *Milagro* (*Miracle*) 1993, Connie Arismendi transforms the Sacred Heart of Catholicism into a sacred image of the female body.

graphic altars dedicated to friends and loved ones, Vargas uses the Heart alone to embody the emotion and passion of her relationships. Connie Arismendi's reason for making art is about creating "images that tell. I think that my images are like prayer.... The whole idea is to evoke.... And what the spiritual power of art can do through images is bridge the gap between people." In her version of the Sacred Heart, Christ's body revealing his heart is replaced by a woman's naked torso dwelling within the heart. This image was buried with the beloved body of Connie's friend Rita, who died of uterine cancer in 1996. For centuries, artists, mostly male, have given divine bodies apprehensible form. Historically, women have interpreted these images according to their own intentions, but now are themselves newly envisioning and creating sacred embodiments of the Divine.

When a woman fully turns to beloved sacred images, she crosses a space between representation and reality. She goes to her altar, completely herself, bodily exposed and ready to receive the love and transformation that is given there in embodied form. Embodiment is the source of her intimacy with the Divine. Together women and their images enter into a "working" relationship that may last a lifetime. Their work is in, and through, and with the body; their spiritual alliance is formulated in experience and entrustment, one body to another.

CHAPTER SEVEN

Barbara Ellmann's *Flower Altar* (1980) is an homage to flowers, the gift most widely given as offerings to deities.

ACTIVATING RELATIONSHIP
ritual gestures and words of power

If the home altar stands as a visual representation of the desire for affiliation, it is the use of ritual and language there that fulfills the altar's potential for actually achieving the benefits of relationship. An altar, by definition, can never merely represent. The altar is a visual model of shared power between a woman and the Divine, but, most important, it is an instrument for the distribution and exchange of that power. It has communication as its *raison d'être* and it fully serves its intended purpose only when the display of powerful things is integrated with powerful actions and words—actions and words that express relationship with the Divine in terms of a woman's beliefs, emotions, needs, and experiences as these unfold and change in day-to-day life.

The need for communication is located in a woman's desire to strengthen her allegiance with personified, embodied deities and to enlist their help in achieving blessed—viable and productive—relationships on earth. Through ritual and speech acts, a reciprocal relationship—giving and receiving between "heaven" and "earth"—is created and recreated in daily devotion; these acts make possible the crossing of the threshold between Self and Other.

Women's private devotion is a refined and quite complex play of power, a mode of purposive interaction, which, as Pat Gargaetas explains, can only happen when the altar becomes "a place where conscious change can be set in motion…. An altar-maker works her altar by focusing her intent, expressing her will, her desire, herSelf. She meditates. She prays. She focuses. She activates images and changes her attitudes. Visibly, palpably, she creates a mental realm and an emotional locus in which connections can be effected, transformations actuated and identity consciously be altered…. I do not merely hold these ideas in my head as theoretical constructs…I play them out on my altar…. And it doesn't matter *how* I make it work, only that I work it."

Like many women who practice Wiccan and Dianic traditions, Renee Dooley consecrates the four elements (the consecration of water is seen here) as part of ritually bringing her altar alive for ceremony and spellwork.

The personal altar always invites dialogue: it engages the maker who, moving beyond the viewing of altar images and objects, begins to use them, to encounter them, to speak to them. The accumulation of objects is matched by the cumulative effect of ritual gestures and spoken words. Here gestures and speech are substantive, if fleeting; they cannot be separated from the material contents of the altar. In combination, these distinct strategies forge an interactive dynamic which is compelling in both affect and effect.

The altar is a prototypical and highly charged performance space, by its very nature reflecting the creative possibilities of symbolic interaction. Nothing is accomplished there without performance. Rituals at the altar reveal women's ability actually to achieve the relationship between distinct entities. Every day, women such as Heather Fox and Sharynne NicMacha rise to their role as self-governing priestesses. Heather's altar to Aphrodite is the site of numerous rituals: "I perform personal rituals, seasonal rituals, moon rituals, healing rituals, and spells, and I do ceremonies and meditations to honor important passages in life, such as birth, menarche, menopause, death…to honor the Goddess and my moontime, to heal Mother Earth and myself, and to promote peace on the planet." Her altar holds various ritual tools such as mirrors, an incense burner, and a silver chalice, essential oils for anointing, crystal balls for divination, a Tarot deck, and a specially-worn moonstone and amethyst headband. Sharynne's altar, too, is a ritual performance space: "I do a great deal of yoga, stretching and breathing exercises for health and meditative reasons, rituals, spellwork, Pagan meditations, singing exercises, and solitary ritual work in front of this altar. It has brought me comfort during my most hopeless times of pain, and has brought me unbounded feelings of bliss and enchantment as well. The more I work with it, for it and through it, the stronger my connection to the Otherworld…people are always immediately drawn to my main altar…it is not just the objects on it…but the sense that I have done so much work in front of the altar, that it is…highly charged."

Sharynne and Heather, like all other altar-makers, perform the work of communication. Communication involves the sharing of codes, codes that when learned and transmitted become the basis for mutual understanding. The altar practice asserts the trustworthiness of women's communication through sacred codes—prayers, orations, songs, and accompanying ritual gestures, such as lighting candles, burning incense, and consecrating the four elements—which invite deities into intimate dialogue with them. Sacred codes are expressed in patterned acts that are to a great extent redundant, but they should never be viewed as passively repetitive, nor as merely obligatory. They are, rather, highly desirable. The rituals of devotion engage women in what Pat Gargaetas views as "an experimental arena where the physics meets the metaphysics." They have an effect, the satisfying effect of daily renewing a meeting with divine resources.

The readiness to relate with the Divine is signaled by simple ritual gestures and the use of instruments purposely designed to enhance affiliation. The regularity of ritual is an expression of steadfastness, of a willed co-dependency. Daily continuity of relationship with the Divine is accomplished through acts that indicate homage and care. Mama Lola "opens" her altars by first attending to the needs of the *lwa* who reside there. She knocks on the door to her altar room to alert the *lwa* that she is coming to them and then follows a regular procedure of greeting, offering, and addressing. Each weekday a different deity is given special attention: "Monday, I spill a little *kleren* [sugarcane rum] for Papa Gede. Then, I speak with him, I say that, after God, I know that he is the one I have as my protector.... Tuesday, I come to spray [*voye*] Florida Water for Elizi Dantò. I light incense. I cense the Petwo altar and spray it with Florida...and speak with her.... Saturday is for all the spirits in general. I speak with all of them." The special nature of Mama Lola's relationships with her *lwa* is marked by ritual gestures that each will appreciate and understand as signs that she knows and cares for them as much as they know and care for her. With similarly easy ritual gestures, Norma Joyce invites the Goddess into her life: "My daily personal rituals are very simple.... I light a candle, thank the Goddess for my life...burn a bit of sage to give the senses a nudge, and ask Her for the coming day to be fruitful and loving."

Mama Lola's altar to Ezili Dantò is filled with ritual activators: a bell from Africa; a calabash rattle; a dish of stones underneath which are the names of people for whom she is "working" the spirits; candles; Florida Water for libation; herb bundles; and small bottles of champagne and gin.

In the initial moments of coming to the altar, a woman uses her body as the first indicator of her intention to communicate with sacred embodiments. The fixed gazing at a beloved image is a moment of intimate engagement, affirming the past and continuing history of relationship with a particular aspect of the Divine. Other physical gestures, such as closing the eyes, raising the arms, clasping the hands, or just sitting quietly suggest respect and openness. Kneeling and bowing reinforce the goal of giving and giving over to the Divine. Celeste West explains the *dasho*, a ritual bow to the Buddha: "First I *dasho*—I bow. I just love this tradition. A lot of people hate it; they think they are losing autonomy by bowing to the Buddha, bowing to something outside. This is where people think of idolatry—they feel they are giving up power—but it's the exact opposite." Acts of supplication are not about giving up power, but about accessing it.

BELOW Mrs. Angelike Manolakis prepares the oil lamp that lights her relationship to the saints on her *eikonostasio*.

Next is the burning of incense or lighting of candles. Ancient and universal in practice, establishing fire and light on an altar expresses the desire to exchange energies between the human and Divine. The smoke of perfumed incense carries that message upward into the space between the visible and the invisible. As Ursula

In making this memorial altar, *Light in the Head* (1994–95), Jan Gilbert created votive candles out of wax-dipped photographs of her friend Jamie, who died of AIDS.

Kavanagh exemplifies, incense is the smoke of communication: "In front of a small, Neolithic statue of a woman, I burn frankincense…and piñon incense. I write out my wishes, desires, fears, problems, and hopes and put them under the statue." Keeping a light is perhaps the most profound ritual symbol of devotion; the flame of a candle is a sign of faith in the ongoing possibility of relationship with the gods. In Greek Orthodox tradition, oil lamps recall the pre-Christian hearth altar. Angelike Manolakis daily renewed the light on her altar: "A light in front of the *eikonostasio* is important…. My light is from oil. Every night I clean it, put in oil, and a bit of water, and I light the wick. Here, in America, most Greeks use electricity. With oil there is a little bit work, a little bit sacrifice; with electricity they only put and forget." The creation of light is particularly crucial to an altar's effectiveness, as Chole Pescina explains, "Yes, because wherever there is even a small light, that person never forgets God." And Sra. Micaela Zapata declares, "Sometimes I don't have enough money for anything, but I have to buy a dollar candle. I just have to buy it."

Putting light on the altar is also a very old memorial gesture. New Orleans artist Jan Gilbert made candles,

BELOW Carolyn Oberst's *Flower Altar* (1992) recognizes the history and potency of flowers as feminine symbols of beauty and life.

melding photos of her beloved friend Jamie, who died of AIDS, into the wax. This was both in remembrance of him and a way of remaining in contact with his energy: "I have lit candles since I was a child.... I was raised Catholic and my grandmother had a little altar where she would light candles every day and put a rose to the Blessed Mother.... My mother still does it.... I light candles to Jamie all the time. Then I had this idea to use my photos of Jamie with candles—the image I wanted was this torso, these outstretched arms of Jamie's.... The outstretched torso became an image of healing for me.... It has a resurrection quality.... Burning his image in the candle released this magnificent process of life and decay.... I am imploring his energy by burning his image."

Mary McIntyre's *Wedding Shrine* (1979) was offered as blessing for the newlyweds.

Regular offerings complement candles and incense in promoting reciprocal relationship with deceased friends or ancestors, and divine beings. An offering is the gesture of a covenant; it is a sign of thanks and a signal that the desired relationship is intact and can be relied upon. Often made in the form of food, flowers, or other natural elements, such as seeds, shells, or water, offerings benefit sacred beings with life-giving symbols of nourishment and beauty. Kathleen Alexander-Berghorn describes the meaning of her offerings to Saraswati: "In offering flowers or sweets to Divine Mother on my altar during worship, I am inspired by the line from the *Bhagavad Gita*, 'If one offers Me with love and devotion a leaf, a flower, fruit, or water I will accept it.' White roses are my favorite flower to offer, as roses are traditionally sacred to the Divine Mother, and white flowers are especially sacred to Saraswati. An offering of candy in a lotus-shaped...dish placed on my altar...becomes *prasad* or sacramental food which, having been accepted and blessed by the Divine, is afterwards eaten with special thankfulness. This practice helps me to remember that all my sustenance, inner and outer, comes from Divine Mother." Both Barbara Ellmann and Carolyn Oberst, artists living in New York, recognize the tradition of the flower offering in their creation of altars

Emphasizing the altar's interactive propensity, Mary Beth Edelson's *Woman Rising* (1974) invited viewers to make offerings by writing their personal testimonies of womanhood and leaving them in "story-telling" boxes attached to the altarpiece emblazoned with feminine power symbols.

dedicated solely to flower imagery. Oberst says, "Flowers seem to have the same kind of special power that altars have: compelling, beautiful, magical, feminine, and religious."

Offerings characterize the interactive propensity of the personal altar. One brings what one has, a symbol no matter how humble, of what one wants to give. Betye Saar reflects upon the spontaneous offerings made at her publicly installed altars: "Sometimes people participate in my altars.... Others have contributed objects, poems, a dance.... This energy coming directly adds power. The giving, adding, becomes contagious." The very fact of the altar's presence, its structural recognizability as a place to receive offerings, encouraged Saar's audience to respond: a part of "me" is added to what "you" have made. Artist Mary Beth Edelson underscored this aspect of exchange in an altarpiece she called *Woman Rising* (1974). "Story-telling" boxes appended to the altar structure allowed viewers to offer a whole spectrum of beliefs and feelings: "They weren't just art pieces. You had to go up to it and get hold of it. Read what others had written. And then of course, the viewer was invited to write her own story and include it for other people to read.... You couldn't just zip through and see the work and be out and know what these pieces were about. You had to stop and interact, participate, and then complete it with your own interaction." In a similar vein, artist Mary McIntyre invited wedding guests to attach blessing notes for the newlyweds on her *Wedding Shrine* (1979).

The altar practice encourages physical interaction; all of the senses are brought to bear on the purpose of devotion. For example, the tactile manipulation of objects—fingering rosary beads, caressing holy images, handling crystals, or cradling a picture of the deceased—brings altar objects alive. Touch is persuasive contact. Altar objects are made subjects through touch. By handling objects, often bringing them off the altar itself and into intimate contact with her body, a woman stimulates a sense of affiliation with what the object represents. Sharynne NicMacha speaks to the kind of intimacy developed at her altar through tactile means: "I'll touch certain items, or hold them in connection with a deep meditation. The deer antlers I often gently touch and caress as they are so sacred to me. I may dip the *athame* [ritual knife used as an instrument of communication] into the sacred well and make sunwise circles over the whole altar if I am trying to gather energy, or counter-sunwise circles to dispel energies. I may touch certain objects with the *athame*, symbolically, I may ring the brass bells to begin and end a ceremony, or to summon certain entities or energies."

Considered effective in bringing divine resources to a peak of potential, particular *power objects* help focus spiritual intentions. According to Margot Adler, the importance of ritual activity is emphasized in Wiccan practice by the attention paid to the "tools of the Craft," which are placed on the altar: "You are basically instructed in the use of all these tools...what an *athame* does, what a wand does, what a censer does." In *orisha* traditions sacred charm bundles called *minkisi* hold and make available the power of a certain deity or force.

Renee Stout's interest in charms, divination, and spell work is exemplified in altars, such as *Memories of the Old Fortune Teller* (1993), which contain traditional conjuring and fortune-telling apparatus.

To help Mexican migrants cross the Rio Grande River into the USA, *curandera* Doña Cristiana used her altar as an oracle, "reading" the river's water—seen in jars on the altar table—to determine safe passage.

Candice Goucher says it was the gift of one such bundle which transformed what previously had been her collection of special objects into an active altar for Ogún: "I think what really activated the accumulation as an altar was a gift from a Yoruban priestess in Trinidad. After a very long ceremony…she presented me with…a bundle of various herbs and items for me to take back home…she was insuring a connectedness with this gift. A spiritual connection…. Ogún instructed the making of this packet. Ogún told them what to put inside. It is a manifestation of Ogún. It *is* Ogún."

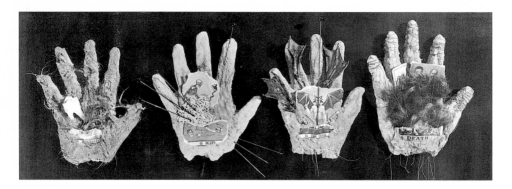

Power objects activate or concentrate connection with divine resources, and are often used in specific types of communication such as spellwork and divination. Power objects help get the business of relationship done. One way that Aina Olomo contacts Shangó is through cowrie-shell or coconut-shell divination, an ancient Yoruban practice which transforms humble cast-offs from nature into message-bearers from the gods. Artist Renee Stout has developed a significant body of altar work devoted to various African and African-American divination and conjuring systems. Stout believes in the power of special objects to assist in enhancing self-determination. She says, "I believe in magic and I'm open to the symbolism in objects and occurrences. The more open I am about these things, the more the magic happens…. If you believe in the charm you have to believe there is power behind it." Doña Cristiana, who lived on the northern Mexican border for decades, practiced "water-gazing," a very old indigenous oracular art, for a new need. Her altar held large jars of river water from the Rio Grande, and each day she "read" the water to help locate safe passage points for people secretly crossing into the United States. The divinatory and oracular nature of certain items on the altar quite dramatically exemplifies the ability of power objects to communicate by symbolically "speaking" in answer to questions posed by the altar-maker.

Artist Paula Lumbard made a series of symbolic "Voodoo hands" as gifts for friends' altars: "Voodoo hands are vehicles for communication with the metaphysical world…. When used to cast a spell, a voodoo hand sits on an altar drawing in the desired energy." At the request of women practicing

Wicca, Goddess Spirituality, and other religious traditions, Ruth Rhoten, an artist working in precious metals and stones, began 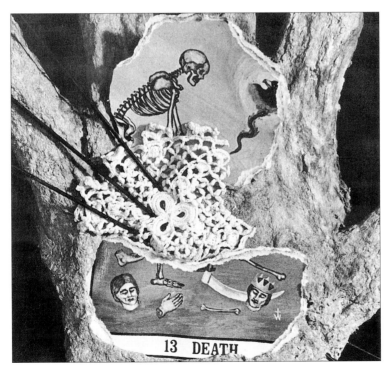 making specialized ritual tools such as wands and *athames*. She also created a power object inspired by her own needs: "I made a woman's knife, a rounded knife—a knife for clearing a pathway.... If I'm working through a particular problem or wanting something to come to me...but something is holding me back, I'll sit in front of my altar with this knife in my hands and light a candle...then I'll...close my eyes and visualize what I want or need.... Holding the knife propels me—because you see it's shaped like a...boat; it's rounded—it pushes through...moving out like a boat cutting through water.... It moves me through."

LEFT Ruth Rhoten created *Knife for Clearing Pathway* (1991) for her own altar. She works in precious metals and stones to make ritual objects commissioned for altars.

Paula Lumbard's *Hand of Death* (1981), seen here in detail, symbolizes the energy of transformation.

13 DEATH

Power objects may end up on an altar by chance. Margallee James was walking on the beach in meditation when she was struck by a desire to write something in the sand. She looked around for an instrument and found a driftwood stick protruding from the sand on the shoreline. The stick was twisted and distorted but it worked perfectly. This humble stick became what Margallee now calls "Venerable Scribe," and it rests behind her altar ready for use again as a tool for spiritual communication.

The manipulation of power objects, the lighting of candles and incense, and the use of initiating ritual gestures are preparatory for the activity that most fully enlivens the altar as an instrument of communication: speaking to the deities. At her altar a woman meets her deities and speaks to them with a sense of assurance in their common desire and ability to sustain life. Personified sacred images lend themselves to speech; familiar images are the intimate subjects to whom speech is addressed.

Through the use of language, the self-created altar becomes a vehicle for self-creation, an instrument for shaping consciousness, and for fulfilling needs and desires. Feminists, among them Dale Spender and Mary Daly, have pointed to the prohibition against women's speech as perhaps the most damaging punishment of patriarchy. Mary Daly says, "Male religion entombs women in sepulchres of silence in order to chant its own eternal and dreary dirge."[1] The home altar's historical longevity is no doubt related to the singular privacy it affords in giving women a place to speak to the Divine without restraint. Women ascribe great efficacy to personal prayer, as Chole Pescina adamantly states: "Let me tell you, prayer is very important for us. For women. The men they should do it, too. But the world was not made for women. You know that. The world was not made for us. I stopped going to church because they accused me of witchery…. But a woman who knows the saints is what? A bad one? No, I tell you we need them. And they know that we have the faith."

Such confidence in knowing and being known by the Divine is the result of regular spoken communication. At her altar a special kind of speech is heard: that of a woman seeking and gaining the power of relationship through *the language of giving and receiving.* Language use at the altar strategically combines prayers of praise and supplication—the language of giving—with conversational outpourings, affirmations, and petitions for blessings and aid—the language of receiving. Praise is formal and figurative, and consists of learned prayers, orations, songs, and chants, which open a line of spoken communication with divine resources. Exaggerated expressions of adoration, respect, obedience, and thanks acknowledge the all-powerful, all-knowing nature of deities and hence their difference from human believers. The competent and regular recitation of orations and chants shows a woman's awareness of the need to maintain propriety in her relationship with divine beings. Of her daily orations to Our Lady of Guadalupe, Chelo Gonzalez says, "When I say my orations to Our Lady I show my respect, my thanks for everything She has done for me. I am willing to do anything She wants."

Chelo learned to pray from her mother. Just as holy statues are passed down in the family from mother to daughter, so are prayers. The devotional traditions of Catholicism, Hinduism, and Buddhism include hundreds of prayers, songs and chants—some of them centuries old—in many different languages. In Catholicism, for example, the saints and various manifestations of the Virgin Mary each have their specific prayers.

Every day Sra. Rocha begins her prayers to the Virgin of San Juan with an oration of praise that in part says, "Oh, Immaculate and Ever Blessed, singular and incomparable Virgin Mary, Mother of God.... Incline, Oh Mother of Mercy, those stars glowing bright from your most merciful eyes." She solicits the Virgin's attention by recounting Her laudable attributes and entreating Her to look down on this believer with Her "most merciful eyes." Sra. Rocha's personal devotion focuses on seeking support in raising her children, so she also recites from memory "A Mother's Prayer," which begins: "Dear Mother, aid my children, May these words be the expression of my heart from the dawn of each day. Oh, Mary! May your blessings accompany them, watch over them, defend them, inspire them, and sustain them everywhere, and in everything." This prayer aligns Sra. Rocha with Mary, mother to Mother.

In her Hindu practice Kathleen Alexander-Berghorn uses the rhythmic, repetitive means of chant and song to declare her devotion to Divine Mother:

"Chanting and singing are an integral part of my devotional labors at my altar. One of my favorite traditional Indian chants, which I first heard Mataji [her teacher] sing at her altar, is a simple hymn to Divine Mother in three of Her aspects: 'Jai Durga Ma Saraswati Mahalakshmi Jai Durga Ma.' Jai means 'victory to.' Singing is sacred to Saraswati and I feel She is present in the song itself."

Newly reclaimed traditions of the Goddess and Wicca also have their formal prayers, but these are more likely to have been recently composed or taken from ancient sources once considered "lost." Several teachers in these traditions have written invocations, blessings, and full rituals which are adapted by practitioners. In Wicca, many women use Starhawk's "Charge of the Goddess," originally written by Doreen Valiente, to open their altars. In part, the "Charge" says, "....I call upon your soul to arise and come unto me. For I am the soul of nature that gives life to the universe. From Me all things proceed and unto Me they must return. Let My worship be in the heart that rejoices, for behold—all acts of love and pleasure are my rituals."[2] Others fulfill their obligations of praise and prayer by writing their own invocations. To honor her focal Goddess, Heather Fox wrote "Aphrodite's Song," a part of which reads: "At My temple sacred healing waters abound, for I am the Great Healer. Come, and step into My magical pools, relax into My loving caress, and feel the pull of My deep waters. Let My liquid touch soothe and heal your aching hearts, your bruised bodies, and your wounded spirits. Sink deeper into the regenerative energy of My womb, and know that I have embraced you with My eternal love, the source of your Wholeness...." Noticeably distinct from conventional religious prayers, both the "Charge" and Fox's invocation invite the deity's presence through first-person verbal personification of Her. The speaker unites with the Goddess; in words, she becomes the Goddess.

In all formal prayers said at the personal altar the loading of speech with metaphor, hyperbole, and repetition is aimed at persuasiveness. As Chole Pescina says of symbolically charged, redolent prayer, "These are the beautiful words that God and the saints like to hear." The language of giving solicits relationship with the Divine and poises the speaker in an attitude of receptivity. It serves as an entry to the language of receiving, the kind of informal, common, and unadorned conversational speech that marks a woman's deepest affiliation with a divine being, the simple "talk" with a deity that explores and daily confirms their relationship with each other.

Whereas formal prayers retain the quality of performed monologues, conversational communion is cast in a dialogue form that gives a woman free rein to speak her mind with the knowledge that she is being heard and actively answered. Having performed her formal orations to the Virgin of San Juan, Gloria Rocha is then, as she says, "Free to speak from the heart": "Then I'm talking with Her, talking like a mother to Mother of God." This "talk" consists of general requests to the Virgin on behalf of her family, but is filled out with the mundane details of her daily life: "I tell Her everything, everything. There isn't much that She doesn't hear from me. Even those silly things like what am I gonna cook for supper.... I get my prayers done with pretty quick so then I'm just talking with Her." Conversation with beloved deities is noted for its impetus toward self-disclosure, for making oneself fully known to the Other, sharing information about one's history, beliefs, hopes, fears, strengths, and weaknesses. Self-disclosure grounds the believer's ability to be fully present as herself with her chosen deities, to ask from them what is needed, and to receive whatever is granted. Petra Castorena neatly summarizes the stages of verbal performance at the altar, and these stages decidedly favor the ultimate progression toward intimacy and equality with the Divine that domestic worship makes viable: "First I say my 'Our Fathers,' my orations, whatever. But then I'm just talking with Her, nagging Her like one of those drunkards who can't stop talking."

Kathy Vargas regularly talks to the Catholic saints of her childhood. She finds in their embodied humanness a desirable, even necessary quality for communication with them: "My best work [making photographs] has come when I've had a good speaking relationship with the deities.... I think for me it's finding a point of contact. Finding a point at which I can feel that they understand what I'm getting at.... All the human ones, the saints, the people who have walked among us, I say, 'You guys better...understand 'cause you've been in this place and you've had choices to make.' And it's about making choices. It's about making the difficult choices that involve more people than yourself. And maybe giving something up in order to make those choices. And that's tough. They've been there. And they are supposed to give us the wisdom and the strength to make those choices. And forgive us when we don't." Vargas's dialogue with the saints is fluid, open, even demanding. Like many other altar-makers, her conversation is about making choices, solving problems, and accepting hardships. In moments of vernacular conversation with their deities, women shape an ethic of concern for themselves and others. The vernacular is unstructured and unrepressed, and suits the task of telling the truth—a woman's version of the truth—to her sacred allies.

Sharynne NicMacha, who at one time followed ritual texts from books on Neo-Paganism, now begins her daily practice with meditation, and then, "I speak either aloud or mentally, or some combination, relying strictly on intuition and the energy and the moment at hand.... I often start out by saying...'Great God and Goddess, be here with me now. I call upon your energy and wisdom to be present this evening, to guide me,' or 'to celebrate this sacred day.' I may stop and start in speaking, as the thoughts come to me. If I ask for something, it is always prefaced with, 'If this is meant to be, help me achieve this goal....' It is all about intent, really. I see the Gods and Goddesses both as greater than us, and I also see them in ourselves....and although I always speak politely and reverently, I feel as if I am talking to a wise friend, someone who loves me...." An altar-maker's intentions are brought forward in strategic shifts between the language of reverence and deference and that of intimacy and feeling. Both are necessary to the goals of devotional practice, but switching is, in the end, always done in the interest of moving from figurative, formal, and coded language to direct talk, which is not restrained by rules or formulas, but rather gives full range of expression to a dialogue with the Divine. If the language of giving is a kind of distancing mechanism that establishes a boundary of respect, the language of receiving then removes this boundary between the human and the Divine.

In conversational talk a woman brings "heaven to earth" on her terms. Just as the altar is full of the visible signs of her history, her relationships, her idiosyncrasies, so, finally, daily talk with the Divine expresses a woman's individuality—her hopes, her dreams, her problems, her complaints. A crucial assumption of power is made within this activity. In revealing herself to the Divine she receives a sense of her worth; she is heard, understood and hence benevolently acted upon by higher powers.

Women are often accused of "talking in circles." The charge trivializes women's speech implying that it is aimless and unassertive. But within the context of the altar practice the phrase "talking in circles" brings to mind a visual diagram of the very way in which the effective mechanics of communication with the Divine are worked out at the altar. "Talking in circles" creates a powerful trajectory that leads from a woman to her deities and back to the woman and others in her care. She sets in motion a cycle that must come "full circle" in order to accomplish its purpose. Activating and daily reactivating the circle of talk between herself and the Divine confirms the closeness of their relationship, and consequently assists in promoting good and productive relationships among humans. At the altar "talking in circles" can be evaluated in terms of the support it yields and the separations it overcomes.

This is the way Margallee James describes the instrumental power of her altar: " 'Taking time to Connect' is…the phrase that comes to mind concerning what happens at my altar. There's a sense of interaction. There's giving and receiving. There's a sharing of energy." Giving and receiving are the constituents of a good relationship. At the altar they are embedded in a continuous flow of communication—in rites and in words—between a woman and her divine allies. Providing a place for the continuity of such communication defines the purpose of the home altar. There, relationship and the terms of relationship are fabricated and refabricated, renewed and revitalized. As Sra. Micaela Zapata emphatically claims, "Every day I'm here at my little altar. Every day. Every day. Even if I'm sick, I still come here. Every day."

CHAPTER EIGHT

Over a decade ago, Nancy Blair began counseling through the organization Adult Children of Alcoholics. Her *Altar to My Child Self* was created at that time, and remains near her bedside to remind her of her recovery from abuses in the past and to keep her grounded in the blessings of the present.

HEALING

restoring body, mind, and spirit

Altars are sites associated with women's belief in the creative, the regenerative, and the restorative. It is no wonder, then, that the tenacious hold of the domestic altar over centuries is vested to a large extent in the access it provides to healing. Healing—of body, of mind, of spirit—is the active result of good relationships between women and their divine allies. It is the manifestation of their inseparability. The oneness of the physical and the spiritual is crucially marked in the evidence provided by healing; it occurs when the gap between Self and Other has been closed, conclusively.

As previously discussed, rituals and speech constitute the performances of "giving and receiving" that activate relationship with divine beings. Healing is an aspect of "receiving," and it has its basis in the particular kind of speech which most characterizes the necessity of keeping an altar: "asking." To be able to petition freely for healing is a woman's ultimate claim that she is known and loved by the Divine. Then all the signs and signals of relationship—the objects arranged, the gestures made, the candles lighted, the prayers said, the praise given, the confessions revealed, the tears cried—strengthen the effort of asking for restoration. As Chole Pescina proclaimed, "Asking is a source of power." This power fortifies a fundamental labor performed at the altar: the movement from problem to solution in the work of living. As Margarita Guerrero affirms, "Here with my saints and the Virgin I have accomplished many things. I have prayed and they answer me. And always I have made things better…for myself and others."

Asking of the Divine is done in the interest of gaining or regaining the productivity of human relationship. The very kinds of requests made through petition are emblematic of a woman's desire to help assure the success of social life, such as appeals to heal the sick, requests for an estrangement to be mended, or for a family home, or a joyous union in marriage, or the birth of a healthy child. A petitioner may also ask as frequently for help in her own self-restoration, since the healing arts practiced at the home altar are always concerned with strengthening both the self and others in relation to the world.

Connie Arismendi suggests that "Women are caretakers and we need help. We are looking for healing and the healing of others. Women look for that.... I think life is really difficult. It's beautiful, but to go through life and to love people and to have that kind of connection is going to result in suffering." The continuity of life is subject to abridgements caused by physical, emotional and spiritual crises, the unforeseen and unavoidable calamities of illness, death, joblessness, and despair—in a word, by *loss*. Asking, advanced by faith, is the means of gaining divine intervention in recovering from loss. In times of crisis, a woman's ongoing relationship with divine allies is tested but also strengthened by the desire for healing. Petitioning seeks the deities' specific attention to her concerns. Asking heightens the terms of their intimacy; asking and then receiving forges a bond of trust.

When she needs help, Vicki Noble comes into relationship with the Tibetan Buddhist goddess called Black Dakini: "When I'm really in trouble, when I really need help—the kind of help you ask the universe for—I go to the Black Dakini.... I just go to her image, over there on the wall.... She carries a knife and a staff with skulls and a trident.... Like Kali, the Black Dakini has to do with rituals...associated with death, rebirth, transformation, letting go. Your ego dying, basically, but it's a merciful kind of having your head taken off.... I feel grateful. Whenever I feel in a process of transformation and at those moments when I feel like I can hardly stand the process—the losses I have to deal with—I'll come into my relationship with her because I know that what I have to do is align with the process, align with the forces of change.... If I come to her...and ask for that help, I get it—it's there anyway.... I can have a conversation with her, let those forces know I'm willing, I'm open."

Petitioning is accomplished in the privacy of the home where intimacy with the Divine is most easily achieved. Petra Castorena says, "I couldn't do this at church. I needed to be here where I could say everything....I have always asked at home. That's where I can cry out." The home altar is always near when a woman needs it, and moreover, it is a self-created place of pure comfort and pure confidence where she can "cry out" with the certainty of being heard.

Without producing results, the home altar would be meaningless as an instrument of communication across the boundaries of the human and the Divine. Petitions find their consequent replies in miracles. There is a tendency to think of miracles as unusual, "unbelievable" interventions, but for altar-makers they are simply the received answers to problems posed by asking. Women speak easily of miracles—those asked for and those received—within the context of relationship, of knowing and being known by their divine helpers. For Chole Pescina asking her favorite saint, San Antonio, was never difficult, nor was the receipt of miracles from him deemed extraordinary : "It's very easy to ask him. It doesn't cost a thing.... He concedes everything to us. All the good things. He's very miraculous. Very, very. What could one ask him that he couldn't accomplish? We ask him with faith and he grants us good things."

Faith is the assurance of relationship with the Divine, and asking in faith positions a woman to receive the benefits of the relationship. She assumes that a response will be given. It is already given in the relationship itself. Petitioning is an act enclosed within the practice of ongoing devotion. This is why the miracle of healing rarely occurs suddenly, and never unexpectedly. That dramatic moments of healing do occasionally occur does not overwhelm the fact that a woman's altar is a place where restoration usually takes place as part of a continuing process of giving and receiving between the human and the Divine. Each day for three years Chelo Gonzalez asked Our Lady of Guadalupe's intercession in curing her husband's cancer. When the disease eventually subsided, the doctor was amazed, but Chelo, who had already accepted the potential for healing in her daily petitioning for it, was simply thankful: "They have given me this miracle and the strength. For that, I give thanks to the Blessed Mother and Our Lord."

The cycle of asking and receiving at the altar is propelled further by promises made to return favor or thanks when a request is granted. Over the period of a year after her husband's recovery, Sra. Gonzalez fulfilled her promise to Guadalupe through the repeated recitation of a prayer of praise to Her. Asking for healing, receiving it, and giving thanks for it encapsulate the purpose of the altar as a place for benevolent, satisfying reciprocation between heaven and earth. Sra. Petra Castorena explains: "I kneel down to pray, I stand up and ask Her. How does the saying go? 'I ask, you give.' I cry out and I ask for whatever I want.... She gives it to me and I give it to Her.... It goes like that. I have fulfilled her promises just as She has fulfilled mine. Just as She does it for me, I do it for Her. That's why I have done washing for Her—washing clothes. So I could take Her an offering of my own sweat. I used to wash and iron and collect the money in a little purse. And then I went and paid Her my promise."

Relationship with the Divine is a working relationship. Many women say that asking for healing and returning thanks is a labor that they perform joyously at their altars. Such labor both determines and satisfies a co-dependent relationship—better, a co-partnership—governed by mutual care and closeness. Petra Castorena and the Virgin each work to meet the needs of the other. Vicki Noble affirms that the power of healing is always dynamic; healing others always promotes self-healing: "It's a call to service. The first mantra I ever got was 'in healing you, I heal myself.' It came like a little song in my head. And it's not narcissistic; it's going in the other direction, in understanding that you get something back from it.... I come to the altar and I turn myself around through thanks. By saying thank you for my life. By giving back."

When engaged for healing, the altar becomes a kind of work table for its maker. Sra. Micaela Zapata called her altar "my business," and there she regularly made petitions on behalf of her family and others who requested her help: "There's that child of mine...he doesn't go to church often. I tell you, when I'm with my saints and he enters—because I close myself in with them—and he comes and he says, 'Mama, I want to talk to you.' And I say, 'What do you want?' He takes his hat right off and enters, asking for this or for that. And it's granted." Implicit in Sra. Zapata's understanding of the altar legacy is the way it serves as a site for accomplishing the work of healing as the work of relationship. Her son comes to her knowing she has shored up affiliations with her saints, and, because she loves her son, she petitions them for him and his requests are granted. Healing power is donated through a system of intimate and interdependent relationships; it is thereby kept in circulation and made continually available for distribution.

Having spent a good deal of time with Mama Lola, Karen Brown realized "…that there is no Vodou ritual, small or large, individual or communal, which is not a healing rite."[1] Mama Lola prepares her altar room each day for the many people who come to her for treatments to help with illness, sour romances, troubled children, unemployment, bad luck, or discouragement. "Sometimes a person has a bad spirit on him and he does not need to go to bed sick. He is feeling like a healthy person, but he feels something is not good. This is not a sickness of the imagination…. I call the spirits to do treatment…. Yes, all this is for treatments. These are sacks of leaves for my work. These are bottles that have medicines in them for my work." Mama Lola's treatments often require great labor—making charms and talismans, creating special baths—and that labor continues: "After you do a big work like that for someone, you don't just forget it. You have to put all your courage into it, pray over that person, pray hard over that person."

Healing can be strenuous, but over time a woman's working relationship with her divine helpers becomes so familiar to her and to them that she may ask with an increasing sense of the restorative power they together create and make available to others. To prove the efficacy of beseeching San Antonio (asked to restore anything "lost", such as love or health), Chole, who knew him so well and had asked his favor many times, pointed to an eye-shaped *milagro* (a small, metallic charm signifying thanks for a specific miracle) hanging on the arm of the saint's image on her altar: "This *milagro* for San Antonio belongs to a man…called Francisco Melendez. He was blinded. They operated on him. As a result he commended himself to San Antonio. He could see only with one eye. [Mr. and Mrs. Melendez] would come to my house, and I said to them, 'Ask Señor San Antonio. He will return the vision of both. Don't just ask for one. He who asks for little deserves nothing. Ask for both.' We helped him and here he is; he drives a car and his tractor at work." According to Chole, healing cannot be evoked out of a sense of scarcity; rather, it is the outcome of assuming an abundant, rich relationship with her favored saint. In countering the "limits" of living, a sense of limitless prosperity is made available at her altar.

For women especially, recourse to divine healing is critical because so often patriarchy and poverty insidiously combine to prevent access to other means of help in times of crisis. Providing an unlimited source of restorative power, woman-centered healing traditions evolve as a strategy for self-sufficiency and survival. The history of European witchcraft could be viewed in such terms, and so could currently effective cults, such as those non-institutionalized and, not surprisingly, unapproved Catholic devotions to a range of "folk saints," including St. Jude, patron of impossible causes; Our Lady of Medjugorje, the recent apparition of Mary in Yugoslavia; and the Mexican healer, El Niño Fidencio. Such devotions involve networks of women who come together in each others' homes to ritually work out spiritual solutions to various material dilemmas. For example, devotees to Niño Fidencio—most of them poor women—create large home altars called *tronitos* (thrones) to house his image and his presence. Regularly, these women engage their *tronitos* in complex *curaciones* (curing ceremonies) that involve shared labor, time, and ritual knowledge. Believers in Niño Fidencio disperse his healing powers by channeling him—becoming him—in trance before his image on the altar. Having learned the tradition of El Niño from her mother Florentina Trujillo, Cuca Borrego passed it on to her daughter who has subsequently passed it on to hers. Four generations of Texas-Mexican women in this family have been aided by the healing arts lent to them by the saint. A friend of Sra. Borrego's, Elodia Jiménez, performs regular healings at her *tronito*. She gives to others a portion of the relief she has received: "When I started getting near the Niño, he take away a lot of suffering from me because I'm a person who suffer a lot since I was a little girl…he start taking me away from all the suffering, and he make me feel good."

In other circles, too, among Wiccans, Goddess Spirituality practitioners, and artists, women in consort with other women create home-based rituals of healing—raising power together to show their care for others, their ability to

Elodia Jiménez has taken a crucifix off her altar to Niño Fidencio, and is seen using it to invoke the Niño's healing powers.

change and be changed. For Wiccans, magic is the means to any transformative experience, including healing. Sabina Magliocco defines magic as "the process of changing consciousness so it conforms to will, to what you want." Healing is assumed to be imminently—and immanently—possible in rituals that ensue from the Wiccan dictum, as stated by Sabina, "Magic follows the path of least resistance."

Physical healing is probably the most widely sought "miracle" of the altar tradition. But bodily restoration figures on a continuum with other kinds of healing, for example the reinstatement of fallen relationships or the making of new ones. In 1980, performance artist Cheri Gaulke and her lover, Sue Maberry, created an altar the centerpiece of which was a portrait of an anonymous bride from the 1950s. She came to symbolize their relationship: "Each time we move, we carry her over the threshold." One of the first rituals performed at this altar involved a desire to transform estrangements. Sue wanted understanding from her parents, who had rejected her for being lesbian, and for Cheri it was her relationship with her best friend, who she was not speaking to: "I used a photograph of her from a performance we had done together. It pictured her face in a nun's habit with mouth taped

Originally conceived for a performance, *Altar for "Death Walk"* (1980) became Cheri Gaulke's and Sue Maberry's home altar, used at times for rituals to heal and transform difficult relationships.

shut. On the tape were the words 'Nothing to Say.' I made an artist book by Xeroxing the photograph and Xeroxing the Xerox ad infinitum until the image disappeared. My intention was that whatever caused us not to speak would disappear. We are now dearest friends again.... She will be the guardian of our children if we should die."

As part of her recovery from childhood trauma related to alcoholism in her family, artist Nancy Blair created her Child Altar featuring a picture of her taken when she was a baby. A therapeutic process of healing her "lost" child-self is encouraged by the visible presence of her portrait conjoined with divine images of protection, compassion, remembrance and transformation. "I spent nearly three years in tears, and painful memories where joy did not burst through the clouds like it does in the movies, but where I could make slow choices rather than find myself compulsively reacting and over-reacting to everything around me based on unresolved issues from my past. One of my first healing acts of power at that time was to set up an altar to my Child Self which I kept on my night stand and continue to keep there today. My Child Altar has changed continually over the years.

BELOW Self-regeneration in terms of career and money is invoked at "prosperity" altars, such as Barbara Ardinger's *Right Livelihood Altar*, made especially to help her achieve her goals as a writer.

In her large-scale altar environment *A Moving Point of Balance* (1985) Beth Ames Swartz created "a journey of healing" for museum-goers who walked through "color baths" keyed to the *chakras* as they viewed seven paintings she made to evoke the power of seven sacred sites she had visited.

However, I continue to use the photo that I first used—a silver-framed photo of me at about nine months old…. In front of the photo are two small identical porcelain owls…. On one side of the photo is a miniature sculpture I made of Hygeia, Goddess of Healing. On the other side are two sculptures of Kuan Yin, Goddess of Compassion. The larger Kuan Yin…carved in jade…was a gift from a very dear woman friend. The smaller Kuan Yin is another of my own creations. My Child Self is protected and guarded by Goddesses that I often call upon in my meditations and prayers. The owls represent Wisdom and the Goddess Lilith, who plays an important role as one of my spirit guides…. Also on my Child Altar I keep a copy of 'The Charge of the Star Goddess.' I often recite this beautiful prayer to my Child Self when I wake up or before going to bed. All of which act as ritual practices for feeling and healing, helping me stay grounded and grateful for my many blessings today."

Many women seek a measure of personal prosperity at their altars—to gain employment, to find a home, or to make any life change associated with self-creation. Author Barbara Ardinger maintains a "right livelihood" altar which rests on her mother's hope chest, and has as its central image a cloisonné bowl she purchased years ago as she set out as a newly divorced single mother.

Among other things in the bowl are wheat from a blue moon ritual, a button that says "Witch and Famous," a sand dollar, a sprig of moneywort and a Susan B. Anthony dollar. Rituals at Ardinger's altar focus on "openness and receptivity, and the bowl is a natural embodiment of those concepts.... I use this altar nearly every morning when I meditate and pray for enrichment via my right livelihood as a writer."

In an assumption of its inherent restorative capacities, the earth's healing power is invoked. In both ancient and contemporary cultures, natural sites—certain wells, waterfalls, groves, trees, caves, mountains, and hills—are in themselves viewed as powerful healing altars. Author Chellis Glendinning, a founder of the Women's Spirituality movement in California in the early 1970s, moved to Chimayo, New Mexico in the mid-1980s. There she discovered the earth as her primary spiritual teacher and her primal source of healing: "At a certain point I just sloughed off everything I knew: Yoga and Buddhism and the Goddess, Jungian material. I just threw it all away and stood face to face in relationship to the natural world. And I said, 'Teach me. I don't know anything. Teach me.' " Chellis had long suffered from abuse in her childhood; her psychotherapy required the painful understanding of her past. But her greatest healing came from an altar which slowly evolved as she walked, mile after repeated mile, the land behind her house. Slowly she learned "how to speak to and listen to the spirits of the land. I learned from my indigenous friends that that is the job of human beings.... At the beginning it took the form of just walking the land, getting to know the land. And then at a certain point I realized there were a lot of potsherds lying around..., they were old pieces. I found this mound and...I began to take the potsherds and put them on the mound. And after a little while I realized I was engaging in a sacred process that mirrored what I was doing in my psychotherapy to heal from trauma.... Taking the pieces that have been forgotten and putting them together. Looking at each piece, examining it, and then putting it down. And I realized, too, that this is what we are trying to do politically in the world, trying to reassemble what mass technology, colonialism, patriarchy—the dominant society—has shattered.... How appropriate that the potsherds became the medium for creating this mandala, this altar."

Glendinning spent the next two years walking and collecting sherds, four at a time, placing them on the mound in the direction they had come from, and daily performing a ritual invocation to the ancestors of indigenous people who live in each of the four quarters: "I would send them the power of this healing place and receive their power and their inspiration." Eventually the beautiful mound altar grew ten feet across. Then suddenly, it was gone. The theft of all the sherds in July 1995 sent Chellis into a temporary state of despair. But she soon realized that she had gained her healing through the process of making her altar—establishing over time a relationship with spiritual resources—not from the fact of its physical existence.

Artists broaden the definition of the altar as a healing instrument by bringing its rehabilitative potential into public settings and effectively inviting the "anonymous" viewer into the experience of transformative healing. Nancy Azara's *Spirit House of the Mother*, carved and assembled from large tree trunks, represents the interior body of the Mother as a healing place. Houselike on its golden outside and womb-like in its dark red interior, Azara says that women who entered it found a "place of vulnerability, where vulnerability is allowed…. One woman described it as experiencing the womb of herself by going inside it. It's an attempt at healing by coming to this wonderful, lush part of the female self." Painter Beth Ames Swartz says: "My sense of intention, whether for personal healing or collective healing, is part of the entire reason that I make art…. Whatever healing skills I have are grounded in who I am: a woman, an artist, a product of Western culture. [But] I believe that we all have the power to heal ourselves and others." Swartz maintains that art should pursue the answer to a critical question: "We have plenty of healing images as precedents in architecture, painting and sculpture, but we've never actually looked at what is transmitted. What is the dialogue that takes place between the image which heals and the person who is healed?" In *A Moving Point of Balance* (1985), what she calls "the most important altar I've ever created," Swartz assembled a large-scale healing environment using as her guiding theme the concept of the seven *chakras* (the ancient Hindu system identifying the energy and healing centers in the human body). Over a four-and-half-year period, Swartz made seven pilgrimages to seven national and

Regina Vater's *Vervê* (1997) (detail shown here) uses corn, beans and rice to create a Mystic Spiral, which is also an eye. The installation is based on the healing metaphysics of Navaho sand paintings and Tibetan ground paintings, and the title in Portuguese translates as "Regard on Seeing."

international sacred sites, and then did a painting based upon her experiences at each one. In the museum setting, Swartz used the paintings to construct an altar environment offering an "intentional journey of healing." Participants walked through seven consecutive, colored light baths, each color symbolically associated with a different *chakra*, and absorbed the power of each painting while standing in its illuminated field of *chakra* energy.

Brazilian-born sculptor Regina Vater made her first altar in 1970 as an act of healing her country: "I wanted to do something hopeful for Brazil because it was such an awful time…. The idea of an altar occurred to me as an urge…. I wanted to do a votive thing, a political thing, a sacred thing. I wanted to combine all these emphases." With friends, Vater went to the beach and made a step-pyramid out of sand. Upon it, among seaweed, driftwood, and other collected gifts from the water, she placed images of the patron saint of Brazil, called Nossa Senhora da Aparecida, who is also associated with Oxumaré (in Candomblé religion the Rainbow-Serpent Goddess of Hope). She left the altar as an offering to the ocean, asking for protection and hope for Brazil. Since then, Vater has made many altars, often composing them with symbolically charged natural materials—feathers, seeds—which signify the immediacy and simplicity of healing through a return to the regenerative powers of the earth.

Requa Tolbert, an artist from New Mexico, created a unique healing environment in the transformation of her old Toyota station wagon into the mobile altar and healing delivery vehicle she calls *Angel Rehab*. Over time she encrusted the inside of the car with amulets, picture cards of Our Lady of Guadalupe and Sheena of the Jungle, flowers, fringes, prisms, and old earrings, and then she painted a mandala on the outside. But the defining altar-like feature of *Angel Rehab* was its use: "…I found myself driving various friends to doctors and driving people who couldn't drive, and we would joke about their being 'rehabilitated by Angels' and how *they* felt better after

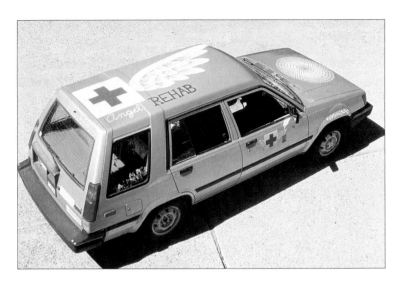

Requa Tolbert's mobile
healing vehicle is called
Angel Rehab and
incorporates an altar
built on the dashboard.

driving with me, and *Angel Rehab* was recognized…. I get a whole new identity: I'm not the nurse any more, or the therapist—I'm just the driver!…Now people give me items for *Angel Rehab*, and I try to drive well—people notice."

Artist Yolda Gutierrez accesses healing power in her dreams. She then makes altars—for example, one called *The Wounded Dove Arises from My Heart* (1992)—as a way to house the power in image form. When Nancy Fried was diagnosed with breast cancer for the second time, she began to make altars dedicated to her recovery. In a series of terracotta works, she framed modeled images of breasts. These were unusual altars, but Fried's immediate recourse to the sacred format is epigrammatic of the home altar's ultimate art. "Five years [after my mastectomy] when I went for a biopsy and they said I had cancer in the left breast, the most amazing thing happened. I saw this…altar of a rose and a breast…. The doctor said the diagnosis and I saw an altar…. So I did the altars…all images of breasts…. I was having radiation and I got badly burned. I made altars of breasts in flames…breasts with ropes tying them down…it was a way of healing…. The breasts in the altars represented the process—they are symbols for loss, for anger, for regeneration…. I mean I didn't do this to make Art; it was about healing."

For many women the "art" of the home altar is about healing. Healing is a process of coming from illness—disintegration—into reintegration of body, mind, and soul. The altar offers a model space for achieving this reconstitution. Belief in the healing work that can be accomplished there is commensurate with a woman's understanding that the altar's threshold between the spiritual and the material is meant to be crossed; it can be crossed, again and again.

Nancy Fried's diagnosis with breast cancer led her to create a series of terracotta altars, among them *Portrait of the Artist* (1992), to facilitate her healing.

CONCLUSION

WOMEN'S ALTARS
a beautiful necessity

This is a most appropriate time to consider women's long-lived tradition of keeping altars at home. We live in an age of instantaneous global communication. Ours is an age of marvels, an age in which computers have made possible the fullest integration of image, word, and sound that the world has yet known. Yet the computer's claim on the future is foretold by something from the past. Long ago, the domestic altar provided the site where binary thinking—the difference and the connection between Self and Other (the 0/1 of human consciousness)—was first conceived. It might be said that the personal computer is "mothered" by the personal altar. Each was invented to enhance the possibilities of human communication and relationship with others. One form has very deep historical roots in the sacred; the other is secular and hardly has a history at all. But they begin to overlap. Evelyn Hall Greiner calls her altar a point of connection with all other altars, "like the Internet. The Internet of the soul." There are many of us whose homes contain both an altar and a computer; in fact, many of us now find our altars *on* our computers.

What are the prospects for the personal altar in the twenty-first century? Evidence suggests that many women are already envisioning millennial meanings for the tradition. Annapurna reminds us that the oldest religious traditions contain seeds of understanding that are useful in projecting the altar's future: "The Hindu goddess of wisdom, Saraswati, is also the goddess of the computer: She is the very power of concentration—she links words and meanings together. She is the power of comprehension. She oversees all writing. She makes what you write understandable to others. She is the source of the computer as altar." The icons on the computer screen have their predecessors in icons of a goddess such as Saraswati.

Susan Gray's computer serves as an altar dedicated to her creativity: "Since I spend a lot of time working on the computer, it is important to me to treat the work I do there—my art and writing—as sacred, and to remind myself to work from my deepest creative self. To that end, I have made an altar space of my computer. On the side of my monitor I have hanging a Goddess...made of handmade papers, found objects and bits of material and string. I have tied small objects of importance to me to some of the strings (a small Carnelian owl for wisdom and protection,...a jade fish for abundance). She is my TechnoGoddess and She protects my computer and my work. My mouse pad is clear and usually holds a photo of a Goddess or sacred space.... My start-up screen is a picture of a Great Horned Owl...and my voice reminding me to open to my deepest wisdom.... When I type my name the computer applauds to remind me to feel good about myself and my work. When I type the word 'spell,' I hear myself saying an affirmation connected to my current spellwork. When I type 'witch' I hear a witch's cackle to remind me not to take it all too seriously."

Artist Katherine Wells creates altars that represent visually her indebtedness to the feminine archetypal potency of the tradition and its ability to capture imagined meanings for the future. She says of one of these altars, called *Our Lady of the Millennium*, that it "reflects my concern with our culture's headlong rush into a technological future.... It is primarily a masculine enterprise and we expect it to be our Savior. At the same time it is, like everything, contained within the ground of the feminine. I have used Our Lady of Guadalupe to represent the container because she has ancient roots, but also real power in the modern world. 'Technos,' this baby, is what is being birthed as we slouch toward a new millennium. The altar is also very personal...because my only child, a son, is a prototype for this new being. His whole soul is bound up in the world of computers and technology with its new icons and arcana, whereas mine resides in the timeless realm of archetype and psyche. Where they interface is the interesting question."

Another artist, Holly Crawford, answers Wells through her creation of a multimedia altar-space, evolving since 1993, called *Offerings*. In various formats, including a physical installation, e-mail and a website, she invites

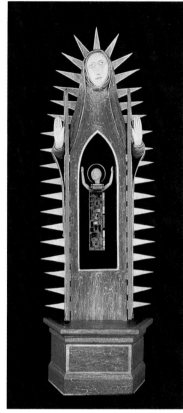

Katherine Wells's sculpted multimedia altars, *La Guadalupana Azteca* (1996, left) and *Our Lady of the Millennium* (1996, right) together summarize the past, present, and future of the women's altar tradition. Within the heart-womb of the ever-present Guadalupe are both her predecessor Coatlicue, the Aztec Mother-Destroyer Goddess, and her future child, Technos, whose body is a computer circuit board.

people from around the world to respond to her request for an offering: "People have offered a part of themselves.... I have asked for offerings from people diverse in occupation, income, geographical location, age, race, religion, and sex.... The time, place, and part of the content are always evolving...transformed by the interactions and additions." In an overwhelming response to her project, she has received hundreds of letters, objects, and ether-messages. Crawford's multi-media approach suggests that one possible future for altar-making is incipient in the current craze for personal websites. Or perhaps, soon, the home altar will find a "second home" available anywhere, anytime, encoded in a pocket-size computer.

Shamaan Ochaum envisions an altar reduced in material form to a singular expression: "I have seen a vision of a pillar with all the symbols of the world's religions carved around the top...and when I came around it there was a blank spot which was a spot for the religion of the future. As I hovered there I saw this image come on to the pillar and it was the image of a rose. And I can see on my altar of the future, a single rose."

It is certainly the case that currently the urge for altars is great, and it shows little sign of abating. Today's marketplace reflects a growing desire for religious images, now avidly collected. Sales of religious antiquities in the 1990s have hit record highs, and the consumption of cheap reproductions of the Virgin, the Goddess, and the Buddha is also off the charts. The Museum of International Folk Art in Santa Fe sells "Shrine in a Bag" for the novice altar-maker who may not have a tradition but wants its trappings. In newspapers and magazines there are lifestyle articles on altars for home beautification. Artist Kanta Bosniak and photographer Diane Porter Goff, who have a business partnership called Sacred Altar-natives, are among several women who give altar workshops and custom-make altarpieces for homes and special occasions such as births and weddings. We are in a period of the personal altar's dramatic reaffirmation.

The eagerness for altars reflects a newly emergent personalized under-standing of the religious that women have practiced for centuries, but which now finds its way into popular culture. A particularly poignant example is the rise of altars among gay men who find in the tradition a way to encourage the healing of loved ones with AIDS, or to meaningfully memorialize them in death. To ease their loneliness, homeless girls in Eugene, Oregon carry portable altars to make them feel at home on the streets. A number of recent museum and gallery shows have explored domestic-altar traditions from various cultures, including Mexican, Indian, and Afro-Atlantic. Even the Catholic Church, which not too long ago prohibited or at least discouraged women's private devotion at home, now invites the practice in certain parishes. Several sets for movies of the 1980s and 1990s—*True Stories, Born in East L.A.*, and *Law of Desire* among them—have featured altars. If the culture at large is catching up with women's practice of the tradition, the home altar may prove itself an ever more effective place of personal encounter with the Divine as we move into a new millennium.

No matter what form the altar of the future takes, women will no doubt always have their particular reasons for keeping the tradition. In the opening pages of this book I suggested that there might be a connection among all women who in the past have kept or now keep the tradition of the home altar. That connection is, I think, a real one. Themes and strategies at work in the legacy of keeping altars—maternal processes, the aesthetic and performance of relationship, the work of healing—reveal the way women use the religious sphere to construct and employ a positive value of their difference. This difference shapes and is shaped by their choice and their determination to live by distinctive beliefs and practices. Certainly, the home altar is a visible sign of the gendered division of labor, but more importantly it marks what Virginia Held calls "the moral division of labor" that informs women's sense of agency.[1] The home altar is a place where a particular reverence for life—an ideology of relationship and regeneration—is put forward as a claim that women make upon the world, where, according to Chelo Gonzalez, "We gather the strength and the faith to continue living. It's marvelous to continue living. Isn't it?" The altar is a woman's access to her kind of power, power shared with and through others, both human and divine. In the full range of its images, symbols, and rituals, the home altar is a "beautiful necessity." It is a sacred and artful instrument for assuring the beautiful necessity of life itself.

Dreams inspire Yolda
Gutierrez's creation of
such altars as *The
Wounded Dove Arises
from My Heart and Is
Cleansed by the Falling
Rain* (1992).

ABOUT THE ALTAR-MAKERS

MARGOT ADLER (New York), a Wiccan, is author of *Drawing Down the Moon: Witches, Pagans, Druids and Goddess Worshippers in America Today* (1979).

KATHLEEN ALEXANDER-BERGHORN (Evanston, Illinois), art librarian, has an MA in Art History, with a special interest in the history and iconography of Goddess worship.

SRA. BERENIECE ALVARADO (San Antonio, Texas), now deceased, erected a large stone-and-cement shrine in her garden, dedicated to Our Lady of Guadalupe and the Virgin of San Juan in gratitude for miracles received from them.

SHELLEY ANDERSON (Minneapolis, Minn.) is a feminist, a worker in the international peace movement, and a member of a lay Buddhist order. She is also a writer, and has published several short stories.

SRA. ANTONIA ANDRADE (Las Milpas, Texas) lives only a few miles from the Texas-Mexican border, and maintains a special altar room for migrant workers.

ANNAPURNA (Portland, Oregon) is the president of SRV (Sarada Ramakrishna Vivekananda) Oregon. She is also an assistant teacher and editor for SRV.

BARBARA ARDINGER (Anaheim, Calif.), born in 1941, maintains principal altars to Brigit, Isis, Athena, and Tara. She is author of *A Woman's Book of Rituals and Celebrations* (1995).

CONNIE ARISMENDI (Austin, Texas), born in 1955, has shown her personal icons and votive objects in many exhibitions. She is inspired by the emotional sincerity and by the physical, non-puritanical nature of Mexican, and medieval and Renaissance European art.

NANCY AZARA (New York), born in 1939 of Italian-American heritage, is a sculptor in wood. Her work since the '60s has sought to reveal the essential female presence within the mystery of the tree.

CRISTINA BIAGGI (Palisades, NY) is a writer and teacher, and the co-author of *Habitations of the Great Goddess* (1994).

NANCY BLAIR (Melbourne Beach, Florida), ceramic artist, recently created a spiral Menopausal Garden and Altar dedicated to Hecate and Kali.

KANTA BOSNIAK (Jacksonville, N. Carolina), fiber artist, clothes designer, and sculptor, works with DIANE PORTER GOFF (Blacksburg, Virginia), photographer, on widely exhibited altar assemblages.

ROSE BUFFALO (Aromas, Calif.), born on the Rosebud Indian Reservation in South Dakota, is a practical visionary, crone, and herbalist. She grows organic corn, fruit, and herbs, and makes "Farm Altars" to express her reverence for nature.

DONNA BYARS (Yonkers, NY) is an artist who uses found natural materials to evoke the shamanistic and unconscious aspects of art. Dreams inspire the mythic content of her assemblages.

MRS. SALLY CANTARELLA (Chase, Texas) is instrumental in maintaining the Sicilian-American St. Joseph's Day altar tradition in her Texas community.

SRA. PETRA CASTORENA (Laredo, Texas), born in 1909, now deceased, raised five children. When one of her sons disappeared in 1975, she placed his picture on her bedroom altar and for twelve years prayed daily for his return.

MIRIAM CHAMANI (New Orleans), priestess, provides spiritual consultation to people from all walks of life at the Voodoo Spiritual Temple in her home.

HORTENSIA AND ELVIRA COLORADO (New York) are sisters who write and produce theater works on indigenous women's history and culture.

HOLLY CRAWFORD (Palo Alto, Calif.), born in 1949, is a painter and printmaker. Her installation, e-mail and Internet altarpiece *Offerings* was begun in 1993.

DOÑA CRISTIANA (Ojinaga, Mexico), now deceased, was a sought-after *curandera* (healer) who lived on the US-Mexican border not far from El Paso.

BETSY DAMON, visual artist/performer, lived in New York for many years. There and throughout the USA and Europe, she

brought the Goddess into the streets in ritual performances such as *7000 Year Old Woman* (1977) and the *The Blind Beggar Woman and the Virgin Mary* (1979).

RENEE DOOLEY (Detroit), in addition to her daily devotional practice, facilitates a Goddess study group, Womansword, and has curated a series of altar exhibitions called "Temple of the Goddess."

ECLIPSE (Providence, Rhode Island), an activist, priestess, and visionary artist, is the founder of EarthCalls Network, an eco-feminist organization.

MARY BETH EDELSON (New York), an international figure in feminist art, continues to find provocative uses for the altar format, as in her late 1990s series of works on the theme of women with guns.

BARBARA ELLMANN (New York), born in Detroit, is a former Teaching Artist at the Lincoln Center Institute.

MELISSA FARLEY (San Francisco), performance artist and psychologist, uses altar-making in group work with women.

HEATHER FOX (Upland, Calif.), born in 1949, is a massage therapist and herbalist, and has studied Goddess Spirituality with Shekhinah Mountainwater.

ROSE WOGNUM FRANCES (Santa Rosa, Calif.), artist, is on the faculty of the Women's Spirituality Program at New College in San Francisco.

NANCY FRIED (New York), born in 1945, is a ceramic artist who has created numerous altar-based works since the 1970s. She says of the women's altar tradition, "It's so old, it works."

SUZI GABLIK (Blacksburg, Virginia), writer, came to altar-making with a desire to "live mythically and symbolically, aligning myself with others working for a renaissance of soul and beauty in everyday life." She is writing a book on her altar to the Black Madonna.

PAT GARGAETAS (Whitethorn, Calif.) wrote her Master's thesis on lesbian-made altars. She has declared herself a Certified *Altar*ed Anthropologist Gone Native Committing Culture with an Attitude.

She says, "I want to advocate altars. I want to advocate for altars. I want to advocate *altar*ations, exploring *altar*ed states."

CHERI GAULKE and SUE MABERRY (Los Angeles) artists, teachers, and mothers of twin girls, were active in the Woman's Building in Los Angeles.

DIXIE FRIEND GAY (Houston), born in 1953, is a painter and sculptor. She belongs to a group who make altars and perform rituals for female rites of passage.

MRS. MARGARET GIACOLONE (Gloucester, Mass.), born in 1912, now deceased, was a member of the Mother of Grace club, Gloucester women of Italian and Portuguese descent who meet to pray, sing, and socialize. Photographer Dana Salvo's exhibition, "Mother of Grace," (1999) documents these women and their St. Joseph's Day altars.

JAN GILBERT (New Orleans), artist, makes altar works that are often elegiac. She is "working with edges—between life and death, photography and painting. The grays of life. The threshold."

JANE GILMOR (Cedar Rapids, Iowa) is Professor of Art at Mount Mercy College and a nationally recognized artist working in photography, video, assembled found objects and metal relief.

JUDITH GLEASON (New York) has documented African and Mexican altar-making traditions in her book *Oya: In Praise of an African Goddess* (1992) and in her video documentary *Flowers for Guadalupe*.

CHELLIS GLENDINNING (Chimayo, New Mexico), one of the founding organizers of the Women's Spirituality Movement in California in the '70s, wrote the Pulitzer Prize nominated *When Technology Wounds* (1990) and *My Name is Chellis & I'm in Recovery from Western Civilization* (1994).

JAY GOLDSPINNER (Greenfield, Mass.), born in 1931, is a professional storyteller of women's tales, and published a coloring book of Goddess images.

SRA. CONSUELO "CHELO" GONZALEZ (Laredo, Texas), born in 1921, has lived in Laredo all her life. She and her husband raised eight children in

their house on San Enrique Street, where they have lived for over fifty years.

LYNN GOTTLIEB (Albuquerque, New Mexico), born in 1949, was originally involved in theater. She became one of the first women rabbis in the USA, and wrote *She Who Dwells Within: A Feminist Vision of a Renewed Judaism* (1995).

CANDICE GOUCHER (Portland, Oregon), born in 1953, teaches African history at Portland State University. Her specialty in African metallurgy brought her to Ogún, the Yoruban god of iron. Her altar holds iron objects—a large bolt from her grandfather's sawmill in Michigan and West African tools.

SUSAN GRAY (Reseda, California) is the author of *Lady of the Northern Light: A Feminist Guide to the Runes* (1993). Practicing spirituality primarily in the Wiccan way, she belongs to two covens, both using group-made altars to focus intentions at their monthly meetings.

EVELYN HALL GREINER (Santa Cruz, Calif.), born in Germany in 1958, gives workshops for women on altar-making, drumming, singing, and sacred art. She is also a counselor for at-risk youth: "I keep an altar for the youth I work with…they are held there, prayed for, and nourished."

SRA. MARGARITA GUERRERO (Laredo, Texas), born in 1897 in San Miguel de Allende, Mexico, now deceased, learned the altar tradition from her grandmother, who also taught her many legends about the Virgin. These she skillfully retold with a feminist relish for the Virgin's point of view, which always conflicted with that of the Church fathers.

YOLDA GUTIERREZ (Houston), born in 1954, holds a BFA in printmaking and ceramics. She makes altars as a place "to give birth to images."

NAGI HASHIBA (Los Angeles) Mother and grandmother, has been involved for decades in the promotion of Japanese culture in Los Angeles.

DONNA HENES (New York), urban shaman, for over 25 years has performed large group rituals for celestial events such as the solstice and equinox. She is the author of *Celestially Auspicious Occasions: Seasons, Cycles & Celebrations* (1996).

MARGALLEE JAMES (North Bend, Oregon). While working as a GED teacher, she remains committed to her spiritual life, reflected in her altar: "It's the physical representation of the center of my life…my connection to the Source."

ELODIA JIMÉNEZ (Lytle, Texas) is a devoted follower of the Mexican "folk saint" Niño Fidencio. She is featured in photographer Dore Gardner's book *Niño Fidencio: A Heart Thrown Open* (1992).

SARAH JOHNSON (Saranac Lake, NY) was born in 1965 in Manchester, England. Married, a nurse, a feminist, and Wiccan, she keeps photos on her altar of herself as a baby and a woman to "remind me that I, too, am Goddess-in-the-flesh."

NORMA JOYCE (Eugene, Oregon), born in 1931, founded an organization WICCA, Women in Conscious Creative Action, in 1983 to promote awareness of women's spirituality issues.

URSULA KAVANAGH (Chicago), an artist born in Dublin, made her first altars in Catholic school to honor the Virgin.

ROSEMARY KELLY (Lodi, Calif.), artist, made a unique series of altars and shrines cut from fabric and sewn.

ANGELA KING (New Orleans), born in Los Angeles in 1954, is director of an art gallery. Raised Catholic, she learned from her mother that "devotion is a life force in defeating oppression."

DAPHNE LESAGE (New Orleans), born in 1954, has created many altars, including a special one made from a gift of jewelry: "It gave me a feeling that I had so much. So, I gave a lot of it away and then made an altar with what was left."

CAITLIN LIBERA (Memphis, Tennessee) author, leads women's spirituality workshops, which include a simple introduction to altar-making.

LAURIE LIPTON, born in 1953, an internationally recognized artist, works exclusively in pencil to make highly detailed, psychologically haunting images.

MAMA LOLA (Brooklyn, New York), who is from a long line of Vodou priestesses, left Haiti for the USA in 1962. KAREN BROWN (New York), a professor of the Sociology and

Anthropology of Religion at Drew University, met Mama Lola while doing an ethnographic survey of the Haitian immigrant community for the Brooklyn Museum in 1978, and wrote *Mama Lola: A Vodou Priestess in Brooklyn* (1991).

PAULA LUMBARD (Los Angeles), artist, expresses feminist spirituality in her paintings, such as *The Triple Muse*.

MARY MCINTYRE (Austin, Texas) dedicated *Wedding Shrine* (1979) "to all marriages, good, bad, or indifferent, past, present, or future."

HAWK MADRONE (Myrtle Creek, Oregon), born in Pennsylvania in 1939 to a Jewish father and a gentile mother, lives in the Oregon mountains, with her friend Bethroot. There she has built a home, cultivated a garden, and made a ritual place for neighboring "land dykes."

SABINA MAGLIOCCO (Van Nuys, Calif.) teaches folklore and anthropology at California State University-Northridge, and has written much on Neo-Paganism.

ANGELIKE MANOLAKIS (Brooklyn, NY) practiced the Greek Orthodox *eikonostasio* tradition until her death.

JOAN MARLER (Sebastopol, Calif.) lectures worldwide on archaeologist Marija Gimbutas's work, and founded the Institute of Archaeomythology to further Gimbutas's approach to scholarship.

DOMINIQUE MAZEAUD (Santa Fe, New Mexico) dedicates all her work—as artist, curator, lecturer, and writer—to "doing art for the earth."

AMALIA MESA-BAINS (Seaside, Calif.) has been making public altar installations in the Mexican tradition since 1976. An instrumental figure in the Chicano art movement, she is also a widely respected curator and educator.

BARBARA BROWN MILLIKAN (Sheridan, Oregon) is a musician, a mother, a massage therapist, and a "mudslinger" (sculptor in clay).

YVONNE MILSPAW (Harrisburg, Penn.) is a folklorist teaching at Harrisburg Area Community College.

JEAN MOUNTAINGROVE (Sunny Valley, Oregon), co-edited the influential feminist spirituality quarterly of the 1970s, *WomanSpirit*. She writes on eco-feminist and lesbian spirituality in *Maize: A Lesbian Country Magazine*.

SHARYNNE MACLEOD NICMACHA (Boston, Mass.), born in 1960, a singer and musician, is deeply involved in Celtic traditions. Her chosen name means "Daughter of Macha," the Celtic goddess associated with horses and fertility.

VICKI NOBLE (Berkeley, Calif.) wrote the guide *Motherpeace: A Way to the Goddess Through Myth, Art and Tarot* (1983, 1994). She is internationally known for her inspirational healing circles and workshops on ritual.

JEANNE NORSWORTHY (Bellville, Texas) is an artist and mother of six children. She paints landscapes on a remote ranch in West Texas.

CAROLYN OBERST (New York), painter, uses her personal altar in conjunction with meditation and yoga.

SHAMAAN OCHAUM (Austin, Texas), a healer, therapist, astrologer, and ritualist, founded the Sacred Hoop Healing Center: "I went to visit the White Buffalo Calf and it was there that I made a deepened commitment to my work as a healer of the Sacred Hoop, to bring the message of White Buffalo Woman and be a Waymaker for the Sacred Hoop."

AINA OLOMO (Austin, Texas), was initiated into *orisha* practice in 1969. Her journey with Shangó has taken her from New York to Trinidad, Florida, and Texas. "The reason *orisha* religion has survived 400 years of oppression and slavery in this part of the world is because it works.... This is not a Sunday go-to-meeting kind of religion. No. No. This is an everyday thing. And it's beautiful. Because you learn who you are. How you fit into the whole scheme of things."

SRA. MARIA PEREZ (Austin, Texas), now deceased, loved to garden, and she often decorated her altar to Guadalupe with flowers that she had grown herself.

SRA. ROMUALDA PEREZ (San Antonio, Texas), and her daughter CASEY COVARRUBIAS (San Antonio, Texas), and other family members, are instrumental in producing the *Shepherd's Play* (*Los Pastores*), a traditional Mexican Christmas play performed outdoors in San Antonio every year for over 100 years.

SRA. SOLEDAD "CHOLE" PESCINA (Austin, Texas), now deceased, learned the home altar tradition from her Mexican grandmother (born *c.* 1820). Chole's gifts as a healer were foretold by her grandmother and mother, who heard her crying out from the womb shortly before her birth in 1896.

CALLIOPE PHOUTRIDES (Portland, Oregon), now deceased, was an early *presbytera* in the USA. The title dates from the fourth century, suggesting women's ordinational status in early Christianity. Now it is the honored title of a priest's wife in the Greek Orthodox Church.

SUSAN PLUM (Berkeley, Calif.) is an artist who works primarily in glass. Her many altar works and votive pieces reflect her long-held interest in Mexican religious folk art and in Our Lady of Guadalupe.

CALELMMIRRE QUELLE (Modesto, Calif.) says her altar is her "secret sanctuary," where she fulfills that "aspect of myself which has always been denied to me in the Christian world, that of priest. "

JAYANTHI RAMAN (Portland, Oregon) from Madras, is a teacher of traditional Indian dance. In the USA she continues to celebrate *Navaratri* (Nine Nights), the ancient Hindu festival featuring elaborate home altars made by women to honor Durga. Jayanthi's personal altar is dedicated to the Hindu god Ganesh.

RUTH RHOTEN (Oakland, Calif.), artisan, has kept her home altar since 1978. At first Goddess-centered, with many images, it now simply holds representations of the four elements. Her altar is used daily for healing, creative work, and what she calls "deep listening," a way of receiving spiritual answers to her life's questions.

SRA. GLORIA ROCHA (San Antonio, Texas), born in 1934, has devoted much of her life to raising her four children with the help of the Virgin of San Juan. She has made regular pilgrimages to the Virgin's shrine, which houses her original image, in Jalisco, Mexico. Her husband is always willing to make the long drive: "I tell him

I'm ready; I need to see Mother of God. And he's ready. He takes me to see Her."

KATE ROMAN (North Highlands, Calif.), born in 1958, spent years seeking spiritual fulfillment in Mormonism, Christian fundamentalism, and a revivalist Scandinavian religion. Finally, she found Wicca: "I'm home. Finding the Goddess ended the fruitless searching."

BETYE SAAR (Los Angeles), an artist of international stature, began making altar works in the early 1970s. Her interest in the mystical and metaphysical has resulted in a rich body of work, combining found objects and spiritual imagery from many cultures. Exhibitions of her work include "Betye Saar: Personal Icons"(1995).

CHERIE SAMPSON (Iowa City, Iowa), artist, built several of her natural habitat altars in Finland in 1998. One was made at the site of a bog.

SHARON SMITH (Austin, Texas), ceramic artist, makes altar-ready votive hearts and vessels in her backyard kiln and firing-pit, and says of her houseful of altars: "The activity of arrangement is like Tai Chi—like my meditation. It's a way of playing, of self-expression, of contentment."

RENEE STOUT (Washington, D.C.), artist, has immersed herself in African and African-American religious traditions, resulting in powerful altar assemblages, such as those in her large-scale installation on the theme of crossroads at the University Art Museum of the University of California at Santa Barbara in 1995.

BETH AMES SWARTZ (Paradise Valley, Arizona), born in New York in 1936, artist, has long been interested in the relationship between art and healing. A series of her paintings, 1996–98, is based on the Chinese healing meditation practice of Shen-Qi.

MARLENE TERWILLIGER (New York), born in 1936, has a PhD in sociology, and taught for twenty years at Marymount Manhattan College. She is a member of The Living Theater.

MARIONE THOMPSON-HELLAND (Bellingham, Washington) makes intuitively-created "Happywomyn dolls," soft-sculpture images of goddesses,

Amazons, and mermaids, found on women's altars throughout the USA.

REQUA TOLBERT (Santa Fe, New Mexico), born into a nominally Methodist family, now calls herself a "generic pagan." A nurse, she moved to Santa Fe, where she emerged as an artist, working in photography and other media.

SHERI TORNATORE (Austin, Texas), born in upstate New York, is an artist whose 1990s explorations include the making of elaborate teapot "altar" assemblages based on *Alice in Wonderland.*

SRA. AURORA TREVIÑO (Laredo, Texas) is known in her neighborhood for the tamales and tortillas she makes every Friday and sells from home.

SRA. VENCESUELA "LALA" TREVIÑO (San Antonio, Texas) was raised on a small vegetable farm in South Texas. Lala and her husband hold a tamale party every 24 December for family and neighbors, to celebrate the birth of Christ.

SRA. FLORENTINA TRUJILLO and her daughter SRA. CUCA BORREGO (San Antonio, Texas), both now deceased, maintained elaborately decorated altar rooms to honor the Mexican "folk saint" Niño Fidencio. Sra. Trujillo was blessed by him in the late 1920s in Espinazo, his home in northern Mexico. Cuca Borrego organized a family pilgrimage to Espinazo every year for the Niño's birthday .

PATSSI VALDEZ (Los Angeles), artist, has created many extravagant, ephemeral public altars, but she is primarily known through her work as a painter.

KATHY VARGAS (San Antonio, Texas), the Visual Arts Director of the Guadalupe Cultural Arts Center, has exhibited her own photographs internationally, and has curated several important exhibitions of Mexican and Mexican-American photography. She has also documented traditional Mexican-American *capillas* (yard shrines) in San Antonio.

JAN WADE (Vancouver), born in 1952, is an artist. In her work *Jazz Slave Ships Witness I Burn* (1996), an ancestral altar with objects representing black diasporic spirituality was ritually burned in the harbor waters of Whitehaven, once an English slaving port.

ERIKA WANENMACHER (Santa Fe, New Mexico) describes the many altars she has assembled since the '80s as "prayers made solid." Her last exhibition this century will be an altar installation dedicated to Kali.

KATHERINE WELLS (Velarde, New Mexico), artist, uses the form of the altar niche because it "reflects the feminine as the ultimate container physically, spiritually, and psychologically."

CELESTE WEST (San Francisco) is a well-known word-witch, independent scholar, creatrix of Booklegger Publishing, and author of *Lesbian Polyfidelity, Or How to Keep Nonmonogamy Safe, Sane, Honest and Laughing, You Rogue* (1996).

YEMAYA WIND (Bandon, Oregon), born in Kent, England in 1946, lives in the country in a wind-powered house filled with altars.

TERRY WOLVERTON (Los Angeles) is a writer, director of plays, and performer. She has used her altar to "gather energy, draw inspiration, fortify myself and other participants" for performances.

NANCY SMITH WORTHEN (Carolina, Rhode Island) lists among sources of inspiration her daughter, a circle of strong women friends, and a beautiful Rhode Island beach called Moonstone.

SRA. MICAELA ZAPATA (Austin, Texas), born in 1890, now deceased, crossed the border into Texas with her grandmother in the 1910 Revolution. They worked for years as field laborers before finding factory work in Austin. As a young woman, Sra. Zapata met Chole Pescina (see above), and they used to go out dancing together. Then they were neighbors in Austin for over 50 years.

LAURIE ZUCKERMAN (Blacksburg, Virginia) "all but abandoned" her career as a painter when she turned to altar-making in the early 1990s, but she approaches her altar aesthetic with a painter's concern for form, color, line, texture, and concept. She regularly spends time "adjusting" her altars: "They are the most fluid part of my home. Altars are intended to be altered, to grow and respond to life's persistent changes."

NOTES

(pp. 6–25)
1 Foster 1967:234
2 Grahn 1997:541
3 Nilsson 1972 [1940]:75
4 Liddell 1925/I:698
5 Demetrakopoulos 1978:62
6 Nilsson 1972 [1940]:73
7 Demetrakopoulos 1978:61–62
8 Downing 1983:95
9 Weitzmann 1978:11
10 Kitzinger 1954:98
11 Herrin 1983:72
12 Brown 1982:296
13 Herrin 1983:70
14 Belting 1994:147
15 Os, van 1994:130
16 Miles 1985:88–89
17 Miles 1985:90

18 Showalter 1985:260
19 Lerner 1979:52
20 Bynum 1986:2, 13, 14
21 Hoch-Smith and Spring 1978:1–3
22 March and Taqqu 1986:67
23 March and Taqqu 1986:67–68
24 Ochs 1983:9–11
25 Daly 1973:156–7

CHAPTER 1 (pp. 26–41)
1 Daly 1973:43
2 Sexson 1982:25

CHAPTER 2 (pp. 42–59)
1 Quaggiotto 1988:313
2 Milspaw 1986:123
3 See, for example, Ghosh 1995

4 Brown 1991:221
5 Weiner 1976:17–18

CHAPTER 3
(pp. 60–77)
1 Lippard 1983:41
2 Christ 1982:75–76
3 Raven 1983:30
4 Raven 1983:41

CHAPTER 4
(pp. 78–93)
1 Gilligan 1982:160
2 Miller 1976:83
3 Gilligan l982:171

CHAPTER 5
(pp. 94–111)
1 Meyer and Schapiro 1978:66–69
2 Lippard 1977:195

3 Stewart 1984:144
4 Gablik 1992:62, 69

CHAPTER 6
(pp. 112–27)
1 Eliade 1963:26
2 Hillman 1975:14, 15
3 Bynum 1986:9

CHAPTER 7
(pp. 128–45)
1 Daly 1973:150
2 Starhawk 1989 [1979]:90–91

CHAPTER 8 (pp. 146–60)
1 Brown 1991:10

CONCLUSION
(pp. 161–65)
1 Held 1987:111

BIBLIOGRAPHY/RESOURCES FOR FURTHER STUDY

Square brackets indicate the printed sources from which altar-maker interview material was taken for this book.

Ardinger, Barbara, *A Woman's Book of Rituals and Celebrations*, Novato, California: New World Library, 1995.

Barstow, Anne, "The Uses of Archeology for Women's History: James Mellaart's Work on the Neolithic Goddess at Çatal Hüyük," *Feminist Studies* 4 (3): 7–18, 1978.

—, *Witchcraze: A New History of the European Witch Hunts*, San Francisco: Harper Collins/Pandora, 1995.

Belting, Hans, *Likeness and Presence: A History of the Image before the Era of Art*, Chicago: University of Chicago Press, 1994.

Blier, Suzanne Preston, *African Vodun: Art, Psychology, and Power*, Chicago: University of Chicago Press, 1994.

Branigan, Keith, "The Genesis of the Household Goddess," *Studi Micenei ed Eego-Anatoliu* 8 (1969): 28–38.

Brown, Karen McCarthy, *Mama Lola: A Voudou Priestess in Brooklyn*, Berkeley: University of California Press, 1991. [*Interview material with Mama Lola cited from pp. 77–78*].

Brown, Karen McCarthy, and Mama Lola, "The Altar Room: A Dialogue," *Sacred Arts of Haitian Vodou*, Donald J. Cosentino, (ed.), 227–39. Los Angeles: UCLA Fowler Museum of Cultural History, 1995. [*Interview material with Mama Lola cited from pp. 227, 229, 236, 237, 238, 239*]

Brown, Peter, *The Cult of the Saints: Its Rise and Function in Latin Christianity*, Chicago: University of Chicago Press, and London: SCM, 1981.

—, *Society and the Holy in Late Antiquity*, Berkeley: University of California Press; and London: Faber, 1982.

Bynum, Caroline Walker, "Women's Stories, Women's Symbols: A Critique of Victor Turner's Theory of Liminality," *Anthropology and the Study of Religion*, Frank Reynolds and Robert Moore (eds), 105–25. Chicago: Center for the Scientific Study of Religion, 1984.

—, "Introduction: The Complexity of Symbols," *Gender and Religion: On the Complexity of Symbols*, Caroline Walker Bynum, Stevan Harrell, and Paula Richman (eds), 1–20. Boston, Mass.: Beacon Press, 1986.

Bynum, Caroline Walker, "The Female Body and Religious Practice in the Later Middle Ages," *ZONE* 3 (1989): 160–291.

Campanelli, Dan, and Pauline Campanelli, *Circles, Groves & Sanctuaries: Sacred Spaces of Today's Pagans*, St. Paul, Minn.: Llewellyn Publications, 1993.

Cash, Marie Romero, and Siegfried Halus, *Living Shrines: Home Altars of New Mexico*, Santa Fe: Museum of New Mexico Press, 1998.

Christ, Carol, "Why Women Need the Goddess: Phenomenological, Psychological, and Political Reflections," *The Politics of Women's Spirituality*, Charlene Spretnak (ed.), 71–86. Garden City, New York: Doubleday & Co., 1982.

Cosentino, Donald, (ed.), *Sacred Arts of Haitian Vodou*, Los Angeles: UCLA Fowler Museum of Cultural History, 1995.

Daly, Mary, *Beyond God the Father: Toward a Philosophy of Women's Liberation*, Boston, Mass.: Beacon Press; and London: Women's Press, 1973.

Demetrakopoulos, Stephanie A., "Hestia, Goddess of the Hearth," *Spring* (1978): 55–76.

Di Leonardo, Micaela, *The Varieties of Ethnic Experience: Kinship, Class and Gender Among California Italian-Americans*, Ithaca, New York: Cornell University Press, 1984.

—, "The Female World of Cards and Holidays: Women, Families, and the Work of Kinship," *Signs: Journal of Women in Culture and Society* 12 (3), 1987: 440–53.

Downing, Christine, "Coming Home to Hestia," *Lady-Unique-Inclination-of-the-Night, Cycle 6*, Kay Turner (ed.), 91–106. Austin, Tex.: Sowing Circle Press, 1983.

Eisler, Riane, *The Chalice and the Blade: Our History, Our Future*, London and New York: Harper and Row, 1987.

Eliade, Mircea, *Patterns in Comparative Religion,* (trans. by R. Sheed) Sheed & Ward: London and New York, 1958; Cleveland and New York: Meridian Books, 1963.

Fairchild, Jill, and Regina Schaare, *The Goddess Workbook: A Guide to Feminine Spiritual Experience*, Portland, Maine: The Great Goddess Press, 1993.

Fewkes, Jesse Walter, *Tusayan Katcinas and Hopi Altars*, Albuquerque, New Mexico: Avanyu Publishing, 1990.

Flores-Peña, Ysamur and Roberta J. Evanchuk, *Santería Garments and Altars: Speaking Without a Voice*, Jackson: University Press of Mississippi, 1994.

Foster, George, *Tzintzuntzan: Mexican Peasants in a Changing World*, Boston, Mass.: Little, Brown, 1967.

Gablik, Suzi, *The Reenchantment of Art*, London and New York: Thames and Hudson, 1992.

—, "Connective Aesthetics: Art After Individualism," *Mapping the Terrain: New Genre Public Art*, Suzanne Lacy, (ed.), pp. 74–87. Seattle: Bay Press, 1995.

Galembo, Phyllis, *Divine Inspiration: From Benin to Bahia*, Albuquerque: University of New Mexico Press, 1993.

Gardner, Dore, *Niño Fidencio: A Heart Thrown Open*, introduced by Kay Turner, Santa Fe: Museum of New Mexico Press, 1992. [*Interview material with Elodia Jiménez cited from p. 64.*]

Gargaetas, Patricia, "Altared States: Lesbian Altarmaking and the Transformation of Self," *Women and Therapy* 16/2–3 (1995):95–105. [*Interview material with Pat Gargaetas cited from pp. 97, 100, 102.*]

Ghosh, Pika, *Cooking for the Gods: The Art of Home Ritual in Bengal*, Newark, NJ: The Newark Museum, 1995.

Gilligan, Carol, *In a Different Voice*, Cambridge, Mass. and London: Harvard University Press, 1982.

Gimbutas, Marija, *The Goddesses and Gods of Old Europe*, (updated edition), Berkeley: University of California Press; and London: Thames and Hudson, 1982.

—, *The Language of the Goddess: Unearthing the Hidden Symbols of Western Civilization*, London: Thames and Hudson; and San Francisco: Harper and Row, 1989.

—, *The Civilization of the Goddess*, San Francisco: HarperSan Francisco, 1991.

Gottlieb, Lynn, *She Who Dwells Within: A Feminist Vision of a Renewed Judaism*, San Francisco: HarperSan Francisco, 1995.

Grahn, Judy, "Marija Gimbutas and Metaformic Theory: Women as Creators of Cognitive Ideas," *From the Realm of the Ancestors: An Anthology in Honor of Marija Gimbutas*, Joan Marler (ed.), 539–47. Manchester, Conn.: Knowledge, Ideas & Trends, Inc., 1997.

Held, Virginia, "Feminism and Moral Theory," *Women and Moral Theory*, Eve Fedder Kittay and Diana T. Meyers (eds), 111–28. Totowa, NJ: Rowman and Allanheld, 1987.

Henes, Donna, *Celestially Auspicious Occasions: Seasons, Cycles and Celebrations*, New York: Perigee/Berkeley Publishing, 1996.

Herrin, Judith, "Women and the Faith in Icons in Early Christianity," *Culture, Ideology, and Politics: Essays for Eric Hobsbawm*, R. Samuel and G. Stedman Jones (eds), 56–83. London: Routledge and Kegan Paul, 1983.

Hillman, James, *ReVisioning Psychology*, New York: Harper and Row, 1975.

Hoch-Smith, Judith and Anita Spring (eds), *Women in Ritual and Symbolic Roles*, New York: Plenum Press, 1978.

Kinsley, David R., *Hindu Goddesses: Visions of the Divine Feminine in the Hindu Religious Tradition*, Berkeley: University of California Press, 1997.

Kitzinger, Erwin, "The Cult of Images in the Age Before Iconoclasm," *Dumbarton Oaks Papers* VIII: 83–149, 1954.

Klein, Anne Carolyn, *Meeting the Great Bliss Queen: Buddhists, Feminists, and the Art of the Self*, Boston, Mass.: Beacon Press, 1995.

Kraemer, Ross Shepard, *Her Share of the Blessings: Women's Religions Among Pagans, Jews, and Christians in the Greco-Roman World*, New York and Oxford: Oxford University Press, 1992.

Lerner, Gerda, *The Majority Finds Its Past: Placing Women in History*, New York and Oxford: Oxford University Press, 1979.

Libera, Caitlin, *Creating Circles of Power and Magic: A Woman's Guide to Sacred Community*, Freedom, Calif.: The Crossing Press, 1994.

Liddell, Henry George and Robert Scott, *A Greek-English Lexicon*, (new edn revised and augmented by H.S. Jones), Oxford: Clarendon Press, 1925–40.

Lippard, Lucy, "Centers and Fragments: Women's Spaces," *Women and American Architecture*, Susana Torre (ed.), 186–97. New York: Whitney Library of Design, 1977.

—, *Overlay: Contemporary Art and the Art of Prehistory*, New York: Pantheon Books, 1983.

March, Kathryn S. and Rachelle L. Taqqu, *Women's Informal Association in Developing Countries*, Boulder, Colo.: Westview Press, 1986.

Mellaart, James, *The Neolithic of the Near East*, New York: Charles Scribner's Sons, 1975.

Mesa-Bains, Amalia, *Ceremony of Spirit: Nature and Memory in Contemporary Latino Art*, San Francisco: The Mexican Museum, 1993. [*Interview material with Amalia Mesa-Bains cited from p. 9.*]

Meyer, Melissa and Miriam Schapiro, "Waste Not/Want Not: Femmage," *Heresies* 4 (1978): 66–69.

Miles, Margaret R., *Image as Insight: Visual Understanding in Western Christianity and Secular Culture*, Boston, Mass.: Beacon Press, 1985.

Miller, Jean Baker, *Toward a New Psychology of Women*, Boston, Mass.: Beacon Press, 1976.

Milspaw, Yvonne, "Protestant Home Shrines: Icon and Image," *New York Folklore* 12 (3&4): 119–36, 1986. [*Interview material with Yvonne Milspaw cited from p. 119.*]

Miska, Maxine, and I. Sheldon Posen, *Tradition and Community in the Urban Neighborhood*, Brooklyn, NY: The Brooklyn Education and Cultural Alliance, 1983. [*Interview material with Angelike Manolakis cited from pp. 22–3.*]

Mookerjee, Priya, *Pathway Icons: The Wayside Art of India*, London and New York: Thames and Hudson, 1987.

Mulcahy, Joanne, "Interview with Calliope Phoutrides", videotape, Portland, Or, 1990. [*Interview material with Calliope Phoutrides cited from tape.*]

Nilsson, Martin P., *Greek Folk Religion*, Philadelphia: University of Pennsylvania Press, [1940] 1972.

Ochs, Carol, *Women and Spirituality*, Totowa, NJ: Rowman and Allanheld, 1983; and London: Rowman and Littlefield, 1997.

Orr, David G., *Roman Domestic Religion: A Study of Roman Household Deities and Their Shrines at Pompeii and Herculaneum*, PhD Dissertation, University of Maryland, 1972.

Orsi, Robert A., *Thank You, St. Jude: Women's Devotions to the Patron Saint of Hopeless Causes*, New Haven: Yale University Press, 1996.

Os, Henk van, *The Art of Devotion in the Late Middle Ages in Europe, 1300–1500*, (trans. from the Dutch by M. Hoyle), London: Merrell Holberton in association with Rijksmuseum, Amsterdam; and Princeton, NJ: Princeton University Press, 1994.

Quaggiotto, Pamela, *Altars of Food to St. Joseph: Women's Ritual in Sicily*, PhD Dissertation, Columbia University, 1988.

Randour, Mary Lou, *Women's Psyche, Women's Spirit*, New York: Columbia University Press, 1987.

Raven, Arlene, "The Art of the Altar," *Lady-Unique-Inclination-of-the-Night, Cycle 6*, Kay Turner (ed.), 29–41. Austin, Tex.: Sowing Circle Press, 1983. [*Interview material with Betye Saar cited from pp. 32, 33, 40; with Terry Wolverton, pp. 29, 39.*]

Saar, Betye, *Secrets, Dialogues, Revelations: The Art of Betye and Alison Saar*,

Los Angeles, California: UCLA, Wight Art Gallery, 1990.

Saar, Betye, *Personal Icons*, Mid-America Arts Alliance, 1995. [*Interview material with Betye Saar cited from p. 9.*]

Salvo, Dana, *Home Altars of Mexico*, Albuquerque: University of New Mexico Press; and London: Thames and Hudson, 1997.

Sciorra, Joseph, "Yard Shrines and Sidewalk Altars of New York's Italian-Americans," *Perspectives in Vernacular Architecture*, III, Thomas Carter and Bernard Herman (eds), 185–98. Columbia: University of Missouri Press, 1989.

Sexson, Lynda, *Ordinarily Sacred*, New York: Crossroad Publishing, 1982.

Showalter, Elaine, "Feminist Criticism in the Wilderness," *The New Feminist Criticism*, Elaine Showalter (ed.), 243–70. New York: Pantheon; and London: Virago, 1985.

Starhawk, *The Spiral Dance: A Rebirth of the Ancient Religion of the Great Goddess*, (revised edn), San Francisco: Harper and Row, [1979] 1989.

Stein, Diane, *Casting the Circle: A Women's Book of Ritual*, Freedom, Calif.: The Crossing Press, 1990.

Stewart, Susan, *On Longing: Narratives of the Miniature, the Gigantic, the Souvenir and the Collection*, Baltimore, Maryland: Johns Hopkins University Press, 1984.

Stout, Renee, *Astonishment and Power: The Eyes of Understanding/Kongo Minkisi—The Art of Renee Stout*, Washington, D.C.: The Museum of African Art, 1993.

—, *"Dear Robert, I'll See You at the Crossroads": A Project by Renee Stout*, Marla C. Berns (ed.), Santa Barbara, California: University Art Museum, 1995. [*Interview material with Renee Stout cited from p. 26.*]

Swartz, Beth Ames, *Beth Ames Swartz 1982–1988*, Scottsdale, Ariz.: A Moving Point of Balance, Inc., 1988. [*Additional interview material with Beth Ames Swartz cited from p. 31.*]

Teish, Luisah *Jambalaya: The Natural Woman's Book of Personal Charms and Practical Rituals*, New York: Harper and Row, 1985.

Thompson, Robert Farris, *Face of the Gods: Art and Altars of Africa and the African Americas*, New York: Museum for African Art, 1993.

Turner, Kay, "Mexican American Home Altars: Towards Their Interpretation," *Aztlán: International Journal of Chicano Studies Research*, 13/1&2 (1982): 309–26.

—, "Why We Are So Inclined: On the Art of the Home Altar," *Lady-Unique-Inclination-of-the-Night* 6 (1983): 4–18. [*Interview material cited: Paula Lumbard, p. 43; Kathleen Alexander-Berghorn, pp. 121–4; Ursula Kavanagh, p. 109; Nancy Smith Worthen p. 111, Jean Mountaingrove pp. 125–29.*]

—, "Home Altars and the Art of Devotion," *Chicano Expressions*, Inverna Lockpez (ed.), 40–48. New York: INTAR Latin American Gallery, 1986.

—, "Mexican American Women's Home Altars: The Art of Relationship," University of Texas, Austin. Dissertation in Folklore/Anthropology, 1990. [*Interview material cited from this dissertation from: Bereniece Alvarado, Antonia Andrade, Cuca Borrego, Petra Castorena, Casey Covarrubias, Consuelo Gonzalez, Margarita Guerrero, Maria Perez, Romualda Perez, Soledad Pescina, Gloria Rocha, Aurora Treviño, Vencesuela Treviño, Florentina Trujillo, Micaela Zapata.*]

—, and Suzanne Seriff, " 'Giving an Altar to St. Joseph': A Feminist Perspective on a Patronal Feast," *Feminist Theory and the Study of Folklore*, Susan Hollis, Linda Pershing and M. Jane Young (eds), 89–117. Urbana: University of Illinois Press, 1993. [*Interview material with Sally Cantarella cited from pp. 97, 105, 107.*]

Wade, Jan, *Epiphany*, Banff, Alberta, Canada: The Walter Phillips Gallery, 1994.

Wadley, Susan S., "Hindu Women's Family and Household Rites in a North Indian Village," *Unspoken Worlds: Women's Religious Lives in Non-Western Cultures*, Nancy A. Falk and Rita M. Gross (eds), 94–109. San Francisco: Harper and Row, 1980.

Weiner, Annette, *Women of Value, Men of Renown*, Austin, and London: University of Texas Press, 1976.

Weitzmann, Kurt, *The Icon: Holy Images, Sixth to Fourteenth Century*, London: Chatto and Windus; and New York: George Braziller, 1978.

PHOTO CREDITS

Page 1 Houston, TX, 1990. Photos George Craig **2** Kyle, TX, 1997. Photo Kay Turner **3** Austin, TX, 1993. Photo Martin Harris **4** New York, NY, 1994. Photo Christopher Burke **5** Austin, TX, 1997. Photo Mary Molina **6** Austin, TX, 1979. Photo Kay Turner **7** Linda Mount-Williams after R.R. Schmidt's drawing in Marija Gimbutas, *The Goddesses and Gods of Old Europe,* updated edition, Berkeley: University of California Press; London: Thames and Hudson; 1982, p. 85. Courtesy of Joan Marler and the Estate of Marija Gimbutas **8** Berlinghiero Berlinghieri, *Virgin and Child with Saints, c.* 1230s. Tempera and gold on wood. 42.8 x 27 cm (16¾ x 10½"). © The Cleveland Museum of Art. Gift of the John Huntington Art and Polytechnic Trust, 1966. 237. **9** Blacksburg, VA, 1998. Photo Diane Porter Goff **10** Shrine with images of Krishna and Radha, 18th–19th century, Indian. Brass. Height 96.5 cm (38"). Courtesy of The Newark Museum, Newark, New Jersey. Gift of Dr. and Mrs. Richard J. Nalin, 1987 and 1988. 88. 480. **11** *above* Linda Mount-Williams after Makarevich in Marija Gimbutas, *The Goddesses and Gods of Old Europe,* Berkeley and London, 1982, p. 72. Courtesy of Joan Marler and the Estate of Marija Gimbutas **11** *below* Linda Mount-Williams after M. Gimbutas in Marija Gimbutas, *The Goddesses and Gods of Old Europe,* Berkeley and London, 1982, p. 81. Courtesy of Joan Marler and the Estate of Marija Gimbutas **12** Coos Bay, OR, 1997. Photo Margallee James **15** The goddesses Demeter and Persephone, Greek, *c.* 500 BCE. Marble relief. Courtesy of The Metropolitan Museum of Art, New York. Fletcher Fund, 1924. 24.97.99. **18** *The Adoration of the Magi,* house altarpiece, South Netherlandish (Brussels), *c.* 1500–20. Painted walnut with lead tracery and rosettes and stamped paper backgrounds. Courtesy of The Victoria and Albert Museum, London. 3264-1856. **20** Joos van Cleve, *The Annunciation, c.* 1525. Oil on wood, 86.4 x 80 cm (34 x 31½"). Courtesy of The Metropolitan Museum of Art, New York. The Friedsam Collection. Bequest of Michael Friedsam, 1931. (32. 100. 60) **26** San Antonio, TX, 1985. Photo Kathy Vargas **28** Austin, TX, 1979. Photo Kay Turner **29** *left* Boston, MA, 1997. Photo Sharynne NicMacha **29** *right* Austin, TX, 1998. Photo Kay Turner **32** Sacramento, CA, 1994. Photo Pat Gargaetas **33** Sheridan, OR, 1998. Photo Barbara Brown Millikan **35** Laredo, TX, 1986. Photo Kathy Vargas **36** New Orleans, LA, 1995. Photo Kay Turner **37** New Orleans, LA, 1995. Photo Kay Turner **38** Chicago, IL, 1982. Photo Ursula Kavanagh **40** Santa Fe, NM, 1990. Photo Herbert Lotz **41** Laredo, TX, 1985. Photo Kay Turner **42** Crystal City, TX, *c.* 1940. Photo Russell Lee. Courtesy of The Library of Congress, Washington, D.C . **43** Wayne, NJ, 1981. Photo Donald Lokuta **44** Provenance unknown, *c.* 1920–30. Photographer unknown. Gift to the author from Mildred Potenza **45** *above* Las Milpas, TX, 1985. Photo Kay Turner **45** *below* San Antonio, TX, 1985. Photo Kathy Vargas **46** *above* Laredo, TX, 1986. Photo Kay Turner **46** *below* Austin, TX, 1988. Photo M.L. Edwards **47** San Antonio, TX, 1986. Photo Kathy Vargas **48** Gloucester, MA, 1996. Photo Dana Salvo **49** Chase, TX, 1984. Photo Kay Turner **52** Portland, OR, 1996. Photo Eliza Buck **53** Brooklyn, NY, 1994. Photo Martha Cooper **56–57** London, UK, 1994. Photos Miki Slingsby **58** Seattle, WA, 1992. Photo Claire Garoutte **59** Houston, TX, 1990. Photo George Craig **60** Aromas, CA, 1994. Photo Robert D. Rainey **62** Bandon, OR, 1995. Photo Kay Turner **65** New York, NY,

1994. Photo Christopher Burke **66** *left* Lake Superior at Duluth, MN, 1992. Photo Cherie Sampson **66** *right* Yonkers, NY, 1992–94. Photo Will Espada **68** San Diego, CA, 1982. Photo JEB (Joan E. Biren) **70** Soquel, CA, 1997. Photo Evelyn Hall Greiner **71** San Antonio, TX, 1989. Photo: Kay Turner **74** San Francisco, CA, 1993. Photo Bob Hsiang. Courtesy of Yerba Buena Center for the Arts, San Francisco **75** *above* Cedar Rapids, IA, 1980. Photo David Van Allen **75** *below* San Francisco, 1978, other sites through 1987. Photo Yolanda M. Lopez **76** Vancouver, BC, Canada, 1994. Photo Cheryl Bellows **78** Coral Gables, FL, 1982. Photo Rose Wognum Frances **81** San Antonio, TX, 1987. Photo Kay Turner **82** Myrtle Creek, OR, 1997. Photo Hawk Madrone **83** Blacksburg, VA,1997. Photo Laurie Zuckerman **84** Austin,TX, 1997. Photo Kay Turner **86** New York, NY, 1991. Photo Nick Gurwitz **88** Palisades, NY, 1996. Photo Cristina Biaggi **90** New York, NY, 1983. Photo Sarah Jenkins **91** Cedar Rapids, IA, 1994–95. Photo David Van Allen **92** Copenhagen, Denmark, 1980. Photo Mary McNally **94** San Antonio, TX, 1986. Photo Kay Turner **96** New Orleans, LA, 1995. Photo Kay Turner **97** Austin, TX, 1979. Photo Kay Turner. **98** San Antonio, TX, 1986. Photo Kay Turner **99** San Antonio, TX, 1986. Photo Kay Turner **101** Austin, TX, 1979. Photo Kay Turner **102** Laredo, TX, 1986. Photo Kay Turner **103** Los Angeles, CA, 1975. Photo courtesy of Betye Saar **106** Los Angeles, CA, 1993. Photo Gia Roland **107** Lorane, OR, 1998. Photo Majik **108** Chase, TX, 1984. Photo Kay Turner **112** Portland, OR, 1995. Photo Kay Turner **116** Austin, TX, 1994. Photo Rodney Florence **117** *above* Blacksburg, VA, 1997. Photo Diane Porter Goff **117** *below* Austin, TX, 1979. Photo Kay Turner **120** Evanston, IL, 1982. Photo Kathleen Alexander-Berghorn **122** Upland, CA, 1996. Photo Heather Fox **124** New Orleans, LA, 1995. Photo Kay Turner **125** *above* Star River Productions, *Anatolian Birthing Goddess,* Melbourne Beach, FL, 1991. Photo © 1991 Nancy Blair. Courtesy of Nancy Blair **125** *below* Austin, TX, 1998. Photo Kay Turner **126** San Antonio, TX, 1995. Photo Kathy Vargas **127** Austin, TX, 1993. Photo Martin Harris **128** New York, NY, 1980. Photo Barbara Ellmann **130** Detroit, MI, 1997. Photo Renee Dooley **132** *above* Brooklyn, NY, 1994. Photo Martha Cooper **132** *below* Brooklyn, NY, 1983. Photo Martha Cooper **133** *above* New Orleans, LA, 1994–95. Photo Judy Cooper **133** *below* New York, NY, 1992. Photo Kerry Schuss **134** Austin, TX, 1979. Photo Mary McIntyre **135** New York, NY, 1974. Photo Eric Pollitzer **136** Washington, D.C. 1993. Photo Renee Stout **137** Ojinaga, Mexico, 1985. Photo Kay Turner **138** Los Angeles, CA, 1981. Photo Mary McNally **139** *above* Oakland, CA, 1991. Photo Ruth Rhoten **139** *below* Los Angeles, CA, 1981. Photo Mary McNally **146** Melbourne Beach, FL,1997. Photo Nancy Blair **153** Lytle, TX, 1991. Photo Dore Gardner **154** *above* Los Angeles, CA, 1980. Photo Cheri Gaulke **154** *below* Anaheim, CA, 1995. Photo Avanti Images **155** *A Moving Point of Balance,* Nickle Arts Museum, Calgary, Alberta, Canada, 1985. Photo Robert Sherwood **158** Austin, TX, 1997. Photo Mary Molina **159** Santa Fe, NM, 1995. Photos Requa Tolbert **160** New York, NY, 1992. Photo Kevin Noble. Courtesy D.C. Moore Gallery, New York **163** Velarde, NM, 1996. Photos Pat Pollard **166** Houston, TX 1992. Photo Yolda Gutierrez **175** Lodi, CA, 1982–83. Photo Rosemary Kelly

INDEX

Page numbers in italics refer to illustrations

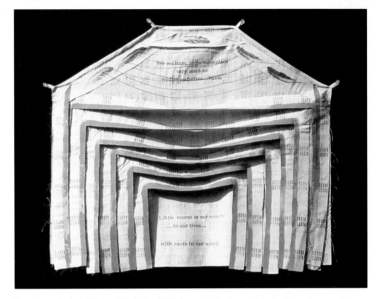

Rosemary Kelly, *Wind Picture #5—Shrine* (1982–83). The lettering reads: "We all have to go someplace very ancient within ourselves...home."